Holding Aces and Eights?

Reno's Potential Threat from Northern California Tribal Casinos

By

Darren Jon Sica

Dr. William Eadington, PhD, Publishing Advisor

University of Nevada Press

December 2001

ABSTRACT

Tribal nations in Oregon, Washington, and New Mexico are already operating Las Vegas style casinos. Nonetheless, Reno/Sparks, Nevada will soon face significant competition from tribal casinos located in Northern California. Nevada as a state receives over a third of its gaming revenue from California. Along with that, California visitors to Reno/Sparks represent 38.2% of their total tourists. However, Reno/Sparks could fare worse than other cities in Nevada. According to surveys performed by the Reno/Sparks Convention Visitor Authority, most visitors to the Reno/Sparks area cite gambling as a primary trip purpose. California tribal casinos could provide a perfect substitute for the short-term visitor to Reno. In addition to that, Reno in the past predominantly catered to gamblers and not emphasized its other amenities.

This thesis will highlight the on-going evolution of the Indian Gaming Regulatory Act, Nevada's tribal casino competition and California's potential impact on Reno/Sparks.

Acknowledgements

Several outstanding souls assisted me in the development and completion of "Aces and Eights". You inspired me throughout the entire process. THANK YOU:

- Grandmother Mary, Grandfather Carmen, Grandfather Don, Aunt Jan, Aunt Kris, Uncle Edward, Father Ron, and brothers-Ryan and Ajeet.
- University of Nevada Professors: Dr. Eadington, Dr. Mitchell and Dr. Gordon.
- My pals: Richard Cerasani, Steve Zawicki, Duke and Molly.

I sincerely appreciate the support and encouragement.

Additional Notes

The writer assumes full responsibility for any errors.

Please direct any questions or comments to the author's e-mail address: DarrenSica@yahoo.com

Table of Contents

Figures and Tables

I. INTRODUCTION

The Indian Gaming Regulatory Act (IGRA) was signed by President Reagan in 1988 in an effort to support tribal self-sufficiency via tribal gaming. Depending on legal interpretation, tribal nations are allowed to offer tribal bingo halls and/or casinos if the state within which they reside allows similar gambling for any reason. Since passage of this act, tribal gaming has become an important presence in many parts of the United States. However, It is likely its greatest presence will ultimately be in the State of California. This poses broad and serious competition for the gaming based economies of Nevada, especially Northern Nevada.

According to IGRA, Types of gaming are broken down into three classes. Class I involves gambling which the tribes perform with their traditional ceremonies; Class II in a broad sense is bingo, or bingo-like games. It also includes non-banked card games. Class III covers everything else, essentially Las Vegas type games, along with pari-mutuel horse racing and lotteries. However, when it comes to Class III gaming, tribes must also sign a compact with a state representative (usually the governor).

This thesis will analyze and evaluate tribal gaming and its evolution in the United States. The main thrust, however, will be on the California tribal gaming market and its estimated potential impact on the casino industry in Reno and Sparks, Nevada. In addition, tribal gaming in several other states will be discussed. The role of California in regards to the overall gaming picture is still undetermined.

Northern California tribal casinos pose the biggest threat to Reno and Sparks, but it should be understood that they are not the only competitive menace to the Silver State. Other Western states (New Mexico, Oregon, Arizona, Washington) also offer tribal gaming. Casinos within these states, especially Washington and Oregon, have probably diverted visitors from traveling to the Reno/Sparks area. Items of interest in these Western states will be discussed. These bits and pieces might indicate trends the Northern Nevada casino industry could find relevant, particularly the observation that politics, not economics, plays a greater role when it comes to tribal gaming. However, economics will ultimately determine the fate of the Northern Nevada casino industry.

For example, it appears that, out of self-interest, New Mexico tribes switched alliance from the Democratic Party to the Republican in exchange for a casino compact agreement, only to be told by the New Mexico Supreme Court that the arrangements were illegal and that IGRA violated aspects of state sovereignty. This set the stage for the New Mexican Legislature (consisting primarily of Democrats) to stonewall the tribes. The New Mexican tribes did, eventually, obtain signed agreements, but not without significant compromises.

Oregon, in contrast to New Mexico, held an opposing viewpoint of IGRA. Oregon figured that if the state allowed any type of gaming for any reason, then they would be under an obligation to negotiate tribal/state Class III compacts. The Oregon lottery does allow a form of sports wagering. Accordingly, two tribes in 1997 negotiated compacts with the state, allowing sports-books, like the type found in Nevada. In addition, the Bureau of Indian Affairs approved the compacts. The only problem these tribes might face is the Professional and Amateur Sports Protection Act (PAPSA) of 1992. This law might not allow the tribes to offer sports wagering as a form of gaming entertainment. The specifics will be discussed and analyzed. No court case has been held; there is yet to be a ruling. Therefore, the issue is still open to interpretation.

Going back to the arena of conflict, the gambling tribes of Arizona, and the Arizona State Department of Gaming continue to take part in an almost classic battle that has been waged since the passage of IGRA. Both sides, the State and the tribal nations, bicker and argue over whose sovereignty is more important.

Washington State, much like Oregon, takes a different approach in contrast to the adversarial relationship found between the Arizona State Department of Gaming and the Arizona Tribal Gaming Regulators Association. In Washington, both the tribes and the state deal with each other on a more equal basis. Washington and Arizona are also compared to Nevada in their approach to casino regulation and control.

In addition, tribal gaming success within the State of Connecticut will be examined. Also, the potential precedents that could have been established in Wisconsin in relation to off-reservation casinos will be evaluated.

A model of Northern California tribal gaming will then be presented, along with the projected impact on the Reno/Sparks gaming economy. This section of the thesis predicts that between 2004-2005, Reno/Sparks will lose over $279,000,000 in gaming revenue due to Northern California visitor diversion to their nearby tribal casinos. Expected loss in revenues could be extended into the future on an annual basis, meaning Reno/Sparks would be without gaming (and associated revenues-lodging, food and beverage, retail, etc.) for years to come.

Finally, the last chapter, titled "recommendations," will focus on the intangible nature of a casino's main product: entertainment. In addition, this chapter will concentrate on ways to improve service. Gaming, in many ways, could be considered a commodity. A casino can set itself apart from the crowd by offering summer pool parties, or by building a dome and displaying must-see laser light shows, but the basic element of entertainment remains the same. The slot machine, craps table, blackjack table, or roulette wheel found in one casino will likely mimic that found in another. A form of differentiation occurs when the staff's service is not only superior to that of the competition's service, but true distinction occurs when memorable experiences are created. Competition in this case could be the casino next door, the carpet joint in Las Vegas, or tribal casinos in Northern California.

California tribal gaming and its impact on Reno and Sparks could be greater or less than the $279 million as predicted in Chapter IV. The last chapter is designed to assist the Northern Nevada casino industry in proactively dealing with a potential huge loss in revenue. However, according to institutional economics, the suggestions in the last chapter (increased market research, importance of employee/patron contact-aka-*moments of truth*, intensified training, and on an aggregate level, cooperation among the casinos in Reno/Sparks) could be hard to implement. This will be explained in the context of path dependency.

II TRIBAL GAMING

It is useful to look at the long history of tribal governments in the context of their relationship to state and federal governments. This information will give a backdrop to understanding where California fits into the overall picture. In addition, historical lessons could also be applied to many of the same tribal/state political situations occurring in California. Also, the experiences of several tribal governments will be analyzed; this will add additional insight to the California state of affairs.

Early History

The first European settlers of North America considered the native people to be members of independent sovereign nations (DeSilva 4). This idea came from Franciscus DeVictoria, an advisor to the Spanish crown in the 16th century. DeVictoria asserted that the indigenous peoples of North America were independent, sovereign, and newly discovered land did not belong to the Europeans, but to the natives. Therefore, DeVictoria set a precedent (4). Accordingly, the only way to acquire land was via treaty (4).

This treatment continued until 1823 (4). The Supreme Court with its fourth Chief Justice of the United States, John Marshall, in essence declared tribes as semi-sovereign, not fully sovereign. Three separate Supreme Court decisions reinforced this view.

The Supreme Court determined in Johnson v. M'Intosh (21 U.S. S. Ct. 543, 1823) that Europeans, by discovering North America, had secured title for their respective governments. Furthermore, the Court decided in Cherokee Nation v. Georgia (30 U.S. S. Ct. 1,5 Pet.1, 1831) that tribal nations would be considered "domestic dependent nations" not "foreign states" (DeSilva 4). Indian reservations obtained a special status with the Federal government: "Their relation to the United States resembles that of a ward to his guardian" (10). The Indians did, however, regain some of their independence in the case of Worcester v. Georgia (31 U.S. S. Ct. 515, 6 Pet 350, 1832).

The court decided in the *Worcester* case that an Indian nation "is a distinct community, occupying its own territory, with boundaries accurately described, in which the laws of a State can have no force" (DeSilva 5). In conjunction with this, the Court looked at past treaties along with British law and decided that prior tribal nations only desired protection from Great Britain. The Indians did not desire to relinquish their sovereignty. This viewpoint set precedent and strengthened the independent nature of tribal nations. Furthermore, the Court also decided that the United States should take the place of Great Britain and provide that same protection. Along with that, an outside Government should not dominate the tribe's activities.

In essence, the court of Chief Justice Marshall fundamentally declared: "The Indian nations, had always been considered as distinct, independent, political communities, retaining their original natural rights" (6). Fourteen years later, the Supreme Court, under the leadership of Chief Justice Roger Taney, held an opposing viewpoint. Taney's interpretation boils down to this: "The native tribes who were found on this continent at the time of its discovery have never been acknowledged or treated as independent nations by the European governments nor regarded as the owners of the territories they respectively occupied" (6).

Taney emphasized Congress's absolute and full authority over Federal/Tribal relationships on tribal reservations. Although Taney held the view that tribal nations were never the true owners of the land they occupied, the ruling of *Worcester* (the idea that state laws hold no validity on tribal land) stayed in place for 100 years. The passage of Public Law 280, in 1953, bestowed to the states of California, Minnesota, Nebraska, Oregon, and Wisconsin the authority over the following on Indian land: criminal violations (as per state law) and issues regarding civil litigation (8).

The Supreme Court case of Bryan v. Itasca County (426 U.S. S. Ct. 373, 392, 1976) further defined Public Law 280's intention. The case centered on the following question: Does PL 280 allow states the power to tax income earned on reservation land? Along with that, can personal property purchased off reservation, but kept on Indian land, be subject to state sales tax? The Supreme Court decided that Public Law 280 did not allow the states to tax Indians. States cannot apply all of their civil/regulatory laws over tribal lands, but can do so on those matters regarding private civil litigation.

The expression "civil/regulatory" which is used in the later cases of *Seminole* and *Cabazon,* originates from *Bryan (*Seminole Tribe of Florida v. Butterworth, 658 F. 2d 310 5th Cir. 1981; California v. Cabazon Band of Mission Indians, 480 U.S. 202-1987). Also the phrase "criminal/prohibitory" emerges from this latter case. Both of these concepts are reiterated in later rulings concerning tribal gaming. Basically, Public Law 280 declares, "Most state laws regulating activities are not enforceable within Indian Lands" (DeSilva9). This idea becomes important in *Cabazon* and Congress's passage of the Indian Gaming Regulatory Act (IGRA).

What about those states not covered by Public Law 280? The 1959 Supreme Court ruling of Williams v. Lee (358 U.S. S. Ct. 217 1959) supported the decision in *Worcester*. That is to say, states could not claim legal control over Indian nations. The court did, however, construct what is known in legal circles as the Williams escape hatch, meaning the tribes would be required to conform to some state authority, depending on the circumstances, such as the criminal offense of murder (DeSilva 9). Nevertheless, a general agreement appeared to have emerged: "The court displayed a likely tendency toward applying the Williams test strictly, and to the benefit of Indian nations whenever possible" (DeSilva 9).

The fact that *Williams* applies in certain cases, but not others, appears to be a major infringement on tribal sovereignty, but the opposite is, in fact, the case. Here is why: the Supreme Court judges, in deciding *Williams,* stated time and again that it forcefully objects to the imposition of state power over Indian nations (DeSilva 9).

Tribal gaming on Indian reservations and the debate over state authority/PL 280's intent begins with the case of Seminole (discussed below), but comes to a climax when a similar case (Cabazon) reaches the Supreme Court.

<u>Seminole Tribe of Florida v. Butterworth, 658 F. 2d 310 [5th Cir. 1981]</u>

Before 1979, there were not more than 10 tribal nations offering bingo enterprises Arendt & Hartman 56). These were small, and low key; much like a church or charity operation. In addition to this they operated once or twice a week with jackpots of nothing more than $100 (56).

The start of tribal reservations offering Las Vegas style casino games began in Broward County, Florida. The Seminole Tribe began offering bingo, but with high stake payouts. Robert Butterworth, Broward County Sheriff, and a passionate adversary of gambling, declared the tribe's operation as unlawful. Florida did allow charitable bingo games, but only if they operated a maximum of twice a week, and with a limited payout of $100. Florida agreed with Butterworth and filed suit against the tribe, however, the U.S. District Court sided with the tribe.

The issue centered on the nature of the law. Indian reservations are subject to state law; but only if it is criminal or prohibitory in nature. In certain cases, if a state law were civil or regulatory, then the tribal nation would not be bound to those laws. The court decided that Florida did not have any authority over the bingo operation in the Seminole reservation because the state permitted bingo, therefore the statute is regulatory in nature.

Florida does have authority over criminal acts on Indian reservations under Public Law 280. The Supreme Court decided civil jurisdiction does apply to Indian land, but only in those cases needed to resolve disputes between Indians and Indians or between Indians and private citizens (Bryan v. Itasca County, supra, 426 U.S. at 383, 96). Furthermore: "The mandate from the Supreme Court is that states do not have general regulatory power over Indian tribes" (Seminole Tribe of Florida v. Butterworth, 658 F.2d 310).

Florida law allows: "Nonprofit or veterans' organizations engaged in charitable, civic, community, benevolent, religious or scholastic works or other similar activities... from conducting bingo games or guest games, provided that the entire proceeds derived from the conduct of such games shall be donated by such organizations to the endeavors mentioned above" (Florida Statute Section 849.093 n5).

Furthermore, penal sanctions exist for violations regarding the operation of bingo. This might appear that any deviance from Section 849.093 would make such an offense criminal. The district court stated this is not the case: "Although the inclusion of penal sanctions makes it tempting at first glance to classify the statute as prohibitory, the statute cannot be automatically classified as such" (Seminole Tribe of Florida v. Butterworth, 658 F.2d 310). In deciding if a law is criminal or regulatory, a simple rule considers the overall public policy of the State of Florida (Bryan v. Itasca County, 426 U.S. 373, 392-1976). If a law conforms to the public policy of Florida, then it is considered regulatory in nature (Bryan v. Itasca County, 426 U.S. 373, 392-1976).

The Florida Supreme Court decided in Carroll v. State (361 So2d 144-1978) and State v. Appelbaum (366 So.2d 443-1979) that "The game of bingo is not against the public policy of Florida" (State v. Appelbaum 366 So.2d 443-1979). Since the law is considered regulatory, not criminal, the Seminoles are free to offer their high stakes bingo games.

The appellate court upheld the decision. The Supreme Court refused to hear the case. The decision of the district court became set precedent.

California v. Cabazon Band of Mission Indians, 480 U.S. 202 (1987)

The Seminole case set a pattern for tribes across the nation: "By 1984 there were 80 bingo parlors operating on reservations in the upper Midwest, California, New Mexico, Oklahoma, and Arizona" (Arendt & Hartman 57). Even though most tribes operated bingo parlors, some reservations diversified, and began offering various types of casino games to their guests. The Cabazon band of Southern California was one of those groups.

The Cabazons offered poker and other games of chance. Just like in Florida, in a case that almost mimicked the Seminole proceedings, the state (along with Riverside County) disputed the Cabazons' casino. Both the state and Riverside County challenged the tribe's offering of bingo. Furthermore, the county wished to apply its statute, prohibiting draw poker. The tribe declared that neither the state nor the county could enforce their gambling laws on tribal sovereign land. The case found its way to the Supreme Court.

The Supreme Court decided that California had no authority to prohibit tribal bingo parlors from operating, under Public Law 280 or under the Organized Crime Control Act (OCCA) of 1970.

According to Public Law 280, California does have authority over criminal acts occurring on tribal lands. However, the State does not have jurisdiction over civil/regulatory issues.

The Supreme Court decided that because California allows bingo to be played by charitable organizations pending certain limitations (such as maximum jackpot), that it is a civil/regulatory issue, and therefore not enforceable under Public Law 280.

The court has, time and again, recognized that Native American tribes preserve "attributes of sovereignty over both their members and their territory" (United States v. Mazurie, 419 U.S. 544, 557-1975). Furthermore, "tribal sovereignty is dependent on, and subordinate to, only the Federal Government, not the States" (Washington v. Confederated Tribes of Colville Indian Reservation, 447 U.S. 134, 154-1980). This does not mean that state law does not apply to Native Americans, but only if congress provides the needed consent. California contended that consent was given under Public Law 280 and the OCCA.

Public Law 280 aimed to promote law and order on reservation land. The court stated: "The act [Public Law 280] plainly was not intended to effect total assimilation of Indian tribes into mainstream American Society. When a State seeks to enforce a law within an Indian reservation under the authority of Public Law 280, it must be determined whether the law is criminal in nature" (California v. Cabazon Band of Mission Indians, 480 U.S. 202-1987). If an action goes against a State's public guidelines, then it is considered criminal, and applicable to Public Law 280.

Clearly, California allows many different forms of gambling: lottery, horse racing, non-banking card games, and charity bingo. Obviously, the State cannot deny the promotion of these games to its citizens. California does not prohibit all types of gambling, but controls and regulates the gambling it does allow. Therefore, gambling in California is a regulatory issue, not a criminal one. The preceding statement is true at least with regard to forms of gambling that are authorized; at the time of the ruling of

Cabazon, other games such as blackjack, and slot machines were against the public policy of the State. Therefore they were criminal.

California argued in Cabazon that high jackpot bingo is a misdemeanor, and in essence a criminal act. Criminal acts can be prohibited on Indian Reservations. The Supreme Court replied: "But that an otherwise regulatory law is enforceable by criminal as well as civil means does not necessarily convert it into a criminal law within the meaning of Public Law 280" (California v. Cabazon Band of Mission Indians, 480 U.S. 202-1987).

Furthermore, the OCCA covers violations of Federal law. States do not have the authority to exercise Federal powers. In essence, California cannot make arrests under OCCA. This appears on the part of California to be a vain attempt to force its laws on Indian reservations (California v. Cabazon Band of Mission Indians, 480 U.S. 202-1987). The Supreme Court goes on to say: "There is nothing in OCCA indicating that the States are to have any part in enforcing federal criminal laws or are authorized to make arrests on Indian reservations that in the absence of OCCA they could not effect (California v. Cabazon Band of Mission Indians, 480 U.S. 202-1987). The court notes, as a matter of fact, encouragement by the Federal government to become self-sufficient through the operation/management of Indian bingo enterprises. The Secretary of the Interior made grants and loans under the Indian Financing Act of 1974 "for the purpose of constructing bingo facilities" (California v. Cabazon Band of Mission Indians, 480 U.S. 202-1987). Also, the Department of Housing and Urban Development and the Department of Health and Human Services "provided financial assistance to develop tribal gaming enterprises" (California v. Cabazon Band of Mission Indians, 480 U.S. 202-1987). If the Federal government decided to shut down bingo operations believing infiltration by criminal elements, they might use OCCA as a tool to do so.

The Federal government's desire to promote economic development on tribal lands is so great that it can even over-ride some state ordinances (Iowa Mutual Insurance Company v. La Plante, ante, p. 9; White Mountain Apache Tribe v. Bracker, 448 U.S. 136, 143-1980). The U.S. Government circumvented state authority because one of the Federal government's primary goals is to "encourage tribal self-sufficiency" (California v. Cabazon Band of Mission Indians, 480 U.S. 202-1987).

Because the Federal government wishes to promote economic development on Indian reservations they, "promote tribal bingo enterprises" (California v. Cabazon Band of Mission Indians, 480 U.S. 202-1987). As already mentioned, several loans and grants were made to tribes per the Indian Financing Act of 1974 for the construction of bingo facilities. Along with that, the Department of Housing and Urban Development and the Department of Health and Human Services have provided financial resources to Indian tribes for the development of casinos / gambling enterprises. These actions demonstrate the U.S. government's interest for self-sufficiency in tribal gaming.

California tries to argue that State law applies to the taxation of cigarettes to non-Indians (Washington v. Confederated Tribes of Colville Indian Reservation, 447 U.S. at 155). If State law applies in this case, then it should apply to tribal gambling. The Supreme Court noted that the Colville tribe purchased a commodity, and then resold it at a discount. There is a difference between buying cigarettes in an Indian smoke shop and leaving, and enjoying the hospitality of a bingo parlor: "They (the Cabazon Band) have built modern facilities which provide recreational opportunities and ancillary services to their patrons, who do not simply drive onto the reservation, make purchases and depart, but spent extended periods of time there enjoying the services the Tribes provide" (California v. Cabazon Band of Mission Indians, 480 U.S. 202-1987). In other words, non-Indians are coming on to the reservation to take part in a recreational activity. Customers are not just buying cigarettes, and then leaving.

The tribes depend on bingo as a source of employment and revenue. The state cannot prohibit bingo on reservation land while permitting it for others throughout the state.

The Supreme Court finishes by saying: "We conclude that the State's interest in preventing the infiltration of the tribal bingo enterprise by organized crime does not justify state regulation of the tribal bingo enterprises in light of the compelling federal and tribal interests supporting them. State regulation would impermissibly infringe on tribal government, and this conclusion applies equally to the county's attempted regulation of the Cabazon card club. We therefore affirm the judgment of the Court of Appeals and remand the case for further proceedings consistent with this opinion" (California v. Cabazon Band of Mission Indians, 480 U.S. 202-1987).

The ruling almost mimicked the Seminole case, but, more importantly, *Cabazon* set a Supreme Court precedent. If a state law forbids a type of gaming, a tribe cannot offer it. Furthermore, a state can take legal action to shut the games down. However, if a state permits a gambling game--bingo, slots, craps, roulette, lotto, horseracing, etc., --then tribes can make the same offerings. The Supreme Court came to their decision on February 25, 1987 (California v. Cabazon Band of Mission Indians, 480 U.S. 202-1987).

This means that if a state authorizes any type of gambling, from lotto to charity Las Vegas Night Casinos (complete with all the games that go along with such casinos), then Indian casinos would be able to operate these same games, notwithstanding restrictive interpretations of public policy by district courts. Needless to say, the state governments of New Jersey and Nevada were not too happy about such unregulated gaming occurring on tribal lands.

Indian Gaming Regulatory Act

In the spring of 1987, Senator Daniel Inoyue (D-Hawaii), Chairman of the Senate Indian Affairs Committee, Morris Udall (D-Arizona), Chairman of the House Interior Committee, along with Democratic Whip Tony Quayle and Senator Harry Reid (D-Nevada) began working on the Indian Gaming Regulatory Act. They faced two basic questions. How would Indian gaming be regulated? Also, how would it be classified?

Many tribes believed, in light of the Cabazon decision, that they would be sole regulators of tribal gaming (Eadington, *Law* 17). This regulation would be done with little or no involvement of the Federal government. The flip side of the coin revealed just the opposite: some states believed the full responsibility would rest in their court (17).

The Senators, in writing the act, decided on three definitions of gaming.[1] Class I would involve traditional/ceremonial games of chance with regulation left totally under tribal control. Class II would include bingo, and non-banking card games. Control of these games would fall under the Tribal nations in collaboration with the Federal government. Class III would include those games that are not Class I or Class II, basically games found in Las Vegas type casinos, along with lotteries and pari-mutuel wagering. Class III required some thought as to its regulatory structure.

Many tribal nations would be reluctant to release all regulation to their respective states (some tribes even wanted control placed in the hands of the U.S. government). At the same time, a number of states could be leery about a model of tribal self-regulation. Senators Inoyue, Udall, Quayle, and Reid decided on what they believed to be a fair and reasonable compromise. Both tribes and states would decide on the regulatory structure via negotiation and mutually agreed compact.

Congress, under pressure from the Supreme Court's decision on *Cabazon*, passed the Indian Gaming Regulatory Act, and President Reagan signed it into law on October 17, 1988 (6). It formed regulations, rules, and guidelines for tribal gaming and created the National Indian Gaming Commission to oversee Class II tribal gaming.

I.G.R.A.'s objective or "Declaration of Policy" (Public Law100-497) is as follows:

(1) To provide the statutory basis for the operation of gaming by Indian tribes as a means of promoting tribal economic development, self-sufficiency, and strong tribal governments.
(2) To provide a statutory basis for the regulation of gaming by an Indian tribe adequate to shield it from organized crime and other corrupting influences, to ensure that the Indian tribe is the primary beneficiary of the gaming operation, and to assure that gaming is conducted fairly and honestly both by operator and players.
(3) To declare that the establishment of independent Federal regulatory authority for gaming on Indian lands, the establishment of Federal standards for gaming on Indian lands, and the establishment of a National Indian Gaming Commission are necessary to meet congressional concerns regarding gaming and to protect such gaming as a means of generating Tribal revenue.

Although the Cabazon case scored a major victory for tribal self-determination and economic independence, some consider IGRA to be a sensitive area in regard to Native American culture.

<u>Tribal Sovereignty and the Potential Disappearance of Culture</u>

Eddie Tullis, Chairman of the Poarch Band of Creek Indians-Alabama, makes the following statement, "It is my opinion that we as a tribal people lost something when

---

[1] Please see, William Eadington (ed.), <u>Indian Gaming & The Law</u> (1998) for IGRA in its entirety, including classes of gaming, and all corresponding regulation.

congress passed the Indian Gaming Act" (Eadington, *Law* 99). Tullis actually views I.G.R.A. as taking opportunity away from Indian tribes. I.G.R.A. as Tullis sees it, will impose restrictions on tribal independence. These constraints will restrict opportunities, and "slice away at (our) tribal sovereignty" (104).

Wendell George, Chairman- Planning Committee of the Colville Confederated Tribes of Washington, also views I.G.R.A. as an attempt to control tribal communities. He has no problem with Class I or Class II gaming. "It maintains our tribal sovereignty. It does not allow the states to control in areas where they were trying to control us" (107). George points out a potential problem with the United States viewing gambling as a privilege. He sees it as an essential element of their Native American culture. The definition of Class III does not take Indian history into account. Native Americans have played ancient forms of dice, cards, and bingo long before the settlement of white men on the continent. George further states, "It is for this reason that we cannot delegate control of our gaming to the state." (108). It should also be noted that George has no problem releasing regulatory control of gaming to the federal government. Even though federal relationships, "have not always been good relationships [. . .] they have been better over the years than working with the states." (108).

Tullis and George are not the only tribal leaders who question the usefulness of I.G.R.A. Harold Monteau, tribal attorney for the Chippewa Cree Tribe of Montana, and later chairman of the National Indian Gaming Commission, views the Act as another step in the direction of integration of Indians into contemporary American culture, further chipping away at tribal autonomy; he equates it to nothing more than "racial genocide" (113). He also believes, and perhaps rightfully so that, "without sovereignty, we do not survive as Indian nations" (112).

Monteau also contends that before I.G.R.A., tribes were free to negotiate agreements with a state as per state and tribal law. Even if I.G.R.A. were found to be unconstitutional, tribes and states would still be able to reach an understanding as to gambling on tribal land. Furthermore, Monteau declares that most of the accountability regarding Class III tribal gaming should be left up to the federal government: "We do not have to have an intrusion of state law enforcement on Indian reservations under the compacts that are envisioned by this Act." (113) According to Monteau, in relation to tribal gaming, law enforcement and regulation should be placed in the hands of the federal government, not only for Class II, but for Class III as well.

Different Interpretations of the Indian Gaming Regulatory Act.

Shortly after the passage of IGRA, William Thompson, of the University of Nevada, Las Vegas, recognized some potential problems with the Act. Thompson stated, at the 1989 North American Conference on the Status of Indian Gambling that there were some flaws in the tribal/state compact process and its compatibility with the United States Constitution. He notes the compact could not be considered a treaty. The 1st article (section 10) of the U.S. Constitution declares: "No State shall enter into a treaty, alliance, or confederation [. . .]". By the same token, tribal governments are not considered foreign, but "domestic dependent nations" (Saum 56). A direct result is that Indian interests are represented by the United States Government (Eadington, Law 40).

IGRA uses the word "compact", which is legally allowed in the Constitution. Article I, Section 10 also proclaims: "No state shall, without the consent of Congress… enter into any agreement or compact with another state…" (Constitution, Article I).

So then, it appears that a State and a Tribal government stand on equal ground and are eligible for compact creation. If this were not the case, then IGRA would not have allowed for it. However, the Constitution does not provide needed instructions for the process. There is, nevertheless an established compact procedure. It comes from page 53 of the U.S. GAO's publication, *Regional Factors in National Planning and Development*. The method consists of five distinct steps (U.S. Government Printing Office, 1935):

(1) Congress authorizes the negotiations of the compact and outlines its purposes.
(2) The state legislature authorizes commissioners representing them to meet and negotiate a compact.
(3) The commissioners meet (under the chairmanship of a Federal representative) to negotiate and sign the compact.
(4) The state legislatures ratify the compact.
(5) Congress ratifies the compact.

According to IGRA, the Executive Branch of the Federal government ratifies the compact, not Congress. Even though Thompson's argument is convincing, it has not yet been used as an argument against IGRA. He ends his discussion on compacts by noting there are several other questions that go unanswered. But perhaps this is the most important: "Who is the final judge of the content and meaning of state law regarding gaming?" (Eadington, *Law* 41). It would appear that answer rests with the courts, particularly the respective Circuit courts and the U.S. Supreme Court.

For example, the 8th Circuit Court in, deciding Cheyenne River Sioux Tribe v. South Dakota, would not allow the tribe to offer casino games, even though the state allowed charitable Vegas nights. Neither could they permit a wagering limit higher than that permitted by state law. The court declared: "such gaming language of South Dakota state law (2710d1B) does not 'require the state to negotiate with respect to forms of gaming it does not presently permit'" (Kelly 530). Also, the State: "…need not negotiate regarding the bet limits because bet limits are established by State law" (530). This represents the latitude that different courts can take to come up with different interpretations. Resolving differences in court opinions can only be achieved by higher court findings and rulings.

Another restrictive court translations of public policy regarding gaming can be found in the following case: Seminole Tribe v. Florida (91-6756, 1993 WL 475999-U.S. District Court, Southern District of Florida, decided September 22, 1993). The court decided that the tribes could not run casino games even though the state allows charity casino nights. Neither could the tribe operate video gambling terminals in spite of their use by the state Lottery.

State's Rights?

There are also some other issues of sovereignty, not concerning tribal nations but with the States of America. A State not desiring tribal gambling only has to convince a Federal court that IGRA violates the United States Constitution, particularly the following sections:

ARTICLE X-The powers not delegated to the United States by the Constitution, nor prohibited by it to the States are reserved to the States respectively, or to the people.
ARTICLE XI-The judicial power of the United States shall not be construed to extend to any suit in law or equity, commenced or prosecuted against one of the United States by Citizens of another State, or by Citizens Subjects of any Foreign State.

The 10th amendment was designed to protect states from the overwhelming power of the Federal Government. It prohibits the U.S. government from forcing the states to do anything not explicitly described in the Constitution. The 11th amendment protects the states from certain lawsuits unless this protection is removed by federal legislation.

Decisions by district courts regarding IGRA's constitutionality have been mixed. The States of Oklahoma, Kansas, and New Mexico tried to use the 10th and 11th amendments in an attempt to keep from agreeing to a compact (Ponca Tribe v. Oklahoma, 37 F.3d 1422-1994). The 10th district court found that congress can nullify a state's 11th amendment protection "by making its intention unmistakably clear in the text of a federal statute enacted pursuant to a constitutional provision that empowers congress with abrogation rights" (Dellmuth v. Muth, 491 U.S. 223, 227-28,105 L. Ed. 2d 181, 109 S. Ct. 2397-1989). In other words, notwithstanding the language of the constitution, congress can void a state's immunity under the 11th amendment. The court also found that congress's intent with IGRA is to nullify a state's 11th amendment immunity, thus subjecting states to suit and forcing them to negotiate in good faith. The court also found that IGRA does not violate the 10th amendment. IGRA only instructs states to cooperate with tribes in an agreeable compact. Congress does not insist on an agreement between states and tribes; it only encourages them to reach an accord.

The 9th circuit court also came to the conclusion that "IGRA's language reveals a clear intent to abrogate the state's 11th Amendment Immunity" (Spokane Tribe of Indians v. Washington, 28 F.3d 991-1994).

The 8th circuit court also agreed with the 10th, and the 9th; The 8th decided the case of Cheyenne River Sioux Tribe v. South Dakota, in doing so they declared: "express provision for the federal jurisdiction over claims under IGRA is sufficient to abrogate the states' 11 amendment immunity" (Cheyenne river Sioux Tribe v. South Dakota, 3 F.3d 273-1993).

However, the Supreme Court reached an alternate decision in Seminole Tribe of Florida v. Florida (517 U.S. 44, 116 S. Ct. 1114-1996). The Supreme Court in this case decided that states are immune from suits brought against them by tribal nations to implement a negotiation under IGRA. Congress does not have the power under the Constitution to impose states to these lawsuits. In concluding, the court decided that congress could not void a state's 11th Amendment exemption concerning areas of Indian Affairs. In essence, this means: "The states could no longer without their consent, be sued in federal district court for a breach of good faith negotiation" (Skibine 403). If a state does not want to negotiate a compact, then they are under no obligation to do so.

Regardless of the interpretations and the opinions regarding I.G.R.A., it appears in some instances to have fulfilled its goal of tribal self-sufficiency.

CONNECTICUT

The Connecticut band of Pequots provides the most successful example of tribal self-sufficiency resulting from the opening of a reservation casino. The Pequots' win, just from slot machines, has steadily increased from $253,108,684 in 1993 to over $731,000,000 in 1999. Please see the graph below

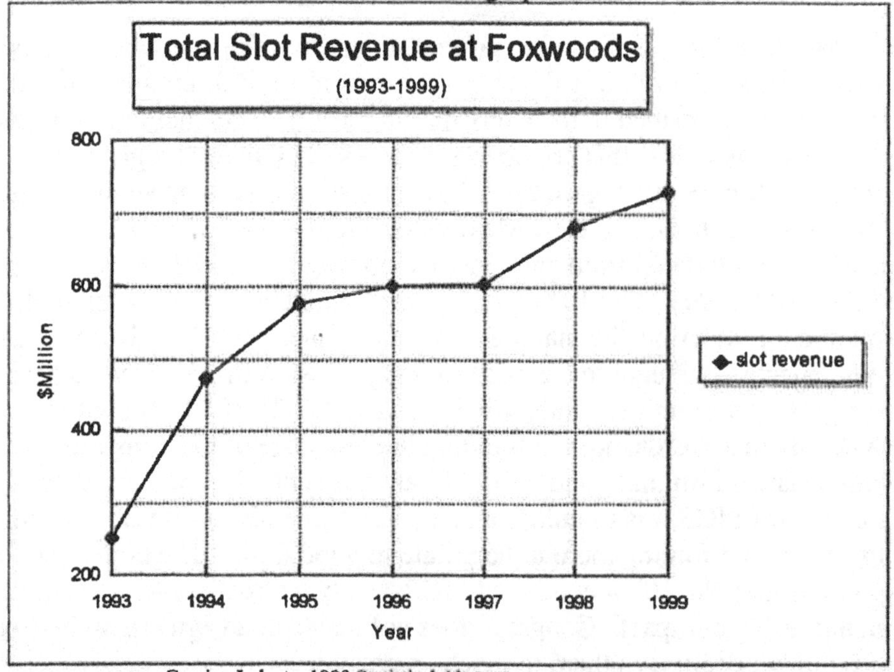

source: Gaming Industry 1999 Statistical Abstract

The Pequot's switch from high-stakes bingo to full-fledged casino began with a desire to reduce teen deaths. Almost 12 Connecticut teens died after prom night in 1986 (Eisler 123). Most of the accidents involved drinking. The local coalition of Mothers Against Drunk Driving (MADD) met to discuss potential solutions to the problem. An idea emerged out of the discussions.

MADD agreed that teens would drink, regardless of the parental warnings. If the kids could be chaperoned at an interesting event for a sufficient amount of time after prom/graduation, then the effects of the booze would wear off. The mothers came to a decision: hold a Las Vegas/Monte Carlo night for the young adults. The games of blackjack, craps, roulette, and poker would be offered, but prizes would not consist of money. The only treasures offered would be items of minimal value, like stuffed animals or key chains. Through much persistence and tenacity a bill allowing post-prom/graduation teen casino nights found its way to Governor William O'Neill's desk. Governor O'Neill viewed the bill with some doubt. However, the teen casinos did not allow for traditional gambling. There was no harm in exchanging play money for a cheap stuffed animal. The bill was signed into law in 1987 on the hope that this would reduce teen drunk driving accidents (Eisler 125). Even though the games would be played with monopoly type funny money, IGRA held an all-important condition, especially for the Pequots. Among other requirements (the Pequots could fulfill), the following was the clincher: "Class III gaming activities shall be lawful on Indian Lands only if such activities are [. . .] located in a State that permits such gaming for any purpose by any person, organization, or entity" (IGRA). The governor, for the purpose of reducing teen drunk-driving deaths, authorized gaming activities.

After the passage of IGRA in October of 1988, the Pequot tribe quickly saw this as an opportunity to negotiate casino table games into their bingo parlor (Eadington, *Law* 34). After all, it was now the public policy of the State to offer a form of casino games. It was no longer a criminal offence, but an aspect of regulation. The Pequots sent a letter to the governor's office on March 30, 1989, requesting Tribal-State negotiations for Class III gaming (Benedict 187). The State's Attorney General, Clarine Riddle, in effect declared the state was ready to negotiate but only if the tribe wanted "to hold Las Vegas Nights in a manner similar to a charitable organization" (188). As already discussed, the winnings would be limited to prizes, not cash. The tribe's attorneys disagreed with Riddle's proposal. Much like the arguments of the Seminole Tribe of Florida and the Cabazons of California, gambling was now regulatory in nature and not a criminal offense. Therefore, the Pequots could negotiate with the State for Class III (Las Vegas style) gambling. Letters went back and forth between the Tribe and the State. Finally, on August 28, 1989, the Pequots filed a lawsuit against Connecticut (188). The state finally realized that, if the status quo held, then casino gambling would come to reservation land.

Still, Governor O'Neill opposed Class III casino gaming for a couple of reasons. Charitable revenue would now flow to the tribe, who were already taking in significant profits from Bingo. But, most importantly, the State of Connecticut could not benefit from casino gambling and a request for tax revenue would be seen as a symbol of bad faith.

Riddle suggested the only way to keep casino gambling out of the State was to nullify and repeal the 1987 charity gambling law. Governor O'Neill did object to Riddle's suggestion. First, it could be viewed as a shifty maneuver that might bring sympathy for the tribe. Due to this, the State Legislature would probably not go for it. Second, the District Court could see this move as evidence of bad faith.

It turned out O'Neill did not have to worry about this headache. He had already decided not to run in the 1988 gubernatorial election. Everything was placed in the lap of the new governor, Lowell Weicker, a proponent of horse racing and an opponent of gambling casinos. He based his opposition to casino gambling on the undesirable elements that might be introduced (crime, prostitution, and drunk driving). Desiring to stop the Pequots from operating a Vegas-style casino, he decided the charity gambling law would have to be repealed. The governor's protests and actions were to no avail; the

Secretary of the Interior, Manuel Luhan, sent word to the Pequots: "Go ahead and start up the [Vegas-style] gambling" (Eisler 140)

The Pequots, seeking counsel, went to speak with the former Chief Enforcement Officer at the New Jersey Casino Control Commission, Michael "Mickey" Brown. Mr. Brown immediately provided the following advice:

- Allow the State to take a primary role in matters regarding employee background checks.
- Permit the Connecticut State Police to enforce criminal law within the casino.

Brown, soon thereafter, accepted employment as a full-time consultant for the tribe. In addition, financing for the enterprise was obtained from Malaysian Billionaire Goh Tong Lim. Foxwood's casino (a name thought up by Tribal Leader, Skip Hayward) was on its way to becoming a destination resort.

Amazingly, Steve Wynn, Las Vegas casino executive, was the catalyst for slots in the Foxwoods. Wynn desired to set up a casino in Hartford, Connecticut, and offer slot machines for his guests. In return, Wynn would be able to offer the State $80 million per year in taxes (179). At this point, September 1992, a side deal was struck between the Pequot tribe and the governor (179). The Pequots would pay the state one of two figures for slot operations in their casino: $100 million per year or 25% of gross slot revenues, whichever was higher. Weicker decided to accept Foxwoods' $100 million guarantee (179). Wynn was out of the picture (at least for the time being), and both sides came to a "win-win" agreement.

Wynn then changed his focus to the city of Bridgeport, Connecticut, at the beginning of 1993 (208). The city more than welcomed the building of a resort casino. Bridgeport's main economic base focused on the defense industry. The main firms in the area, Pratt & Whitney and Sikorsky Helicopters, were in severe financial difficulty. In addition, the city fired its street sweepers, closed its snowplowing operations, laid off its lifeguards, cut senior citizen services, and still could not balance its $308 million budget (208). Also, 15% of the city's residents were on welfare (208). Wynn collaborated with Mary Fritz, chairwomen of the Connecticut House of Representatives Public Safety Committee (209). She put together a bill that would legalize Wynn's casino. The bill was intended to obtain the backing of both unions and minority groups. Most of the construction work, 75%, would be guaranteed to State contractors (209). Also, one-fifth of the casino employees would be hired from State welfare rolls (209).

The Pequots realized it could be in their best interest to team up with their long time enemy, the Mohegan Tribe. This agreement would keep Wynn out of the gaming business in Connecticut. Early in 1994, a meeting was held between the State, the Pequots, and the Mohegans; all three parties came to what appeared to be a win-win-win arrangement.

- A Mohegan compact was drafted, almost identical to the Pequot's. The Mohegans, however, only had to provide the State with a minimum payment of $80 million per year (216). A key provision stayed the same in both agreements: "If a non-Indian casino were allowed to open, the [slot] payments would no longer be required" (216).

- This guaranteed Connecticut minimum yearly payments of $180 million per year. If Wynn built a casino, then these payments would no longer be required. Wynn would not be likely to top this huge windfall for the State.

The Pequots and Wynn met in Hartford to make their proposals for the Bridgeport casino on September 13, 1995 (223). By this time, Weicker had vacated the governor's office and John Rowland took his place. Governor Rowland supported the Bridgeport casino project. More than likely, it appeared a Vegas-style resort would be built in Bridgeport.

Wynn declared his proposal would create 10,500 new jobs and generate a minimum annual amount of $240 million in taxes for the state and the city (223). Wynn, however, could not guarantee this tax revenue. The Pequots, on the other hand, acknowledging their success at Foxwoods, agreed to pay the following: "16% of all casino revenues to the state and 10% of revenues to a Bridgeport Economic Development Fund" (224). They would still pay their 25% fee for their use of slots [at Foxwoods]. The Pequots and Mohegans could easily guarantee the State $180 million per year in revenues. The State expected that a Pequot casino in Bridgeport could, without any difficulty, produce more than $60 million in tax revenue. This would surpass Wynn's proposal. Keep in mind: if Wynn opened a casino, then the tribes would not have to pay a dime to the state.

The governor announced his decision on October 2, 1995 (224). Rowland sought approval from the legislature for a casino at Bridgeport, built by the Pequots. The tribe could not lose, based on whatever came to pass. It was not likely Wynn could endanger the economic well being of the tribe; that danger was removed. If the State Legislature went along with the governor's plan, the Pequots would have a gambling casino 60 miles from heavily populated New York City.

The deal with the Mohegans was designed to keep a casino out of Bridgeport. Now, the Pequots were planning on building a casino in Bridgeport and stealing a majority of the Mohegan's business from New York City. Needless to say, the Mohegan Tribe was not too happy about this arrangement, and pointed out a clause in their compact that basically stated: "The Mohegans make payments if and only if casino gambling is restricted to Indian Lands" (226). On November 25, 1995, the State Senate voted 24 to 10 against the Pequots building a casino in Bridgeport (229).

WISCONSIN

Even though tribal casinos operated in Wisconsin before Connecticut, the Menominee Tribe of Wisconsin, in an attempt to perhaps imitate and even surpass the prosperity of the Pequots sought to obtain land in trust (by the Federal Government) for an off- reservation casino located adjacent to two major population centers. The political maneuvering that took place could set guidelines for states/tribes in other states going through similar negotiations.

The Menominee tribe began operating slot machines in 1987; they were the first Wisconsin tribe to do so (Light & Rand 352). In accordance with IGRA, by 1992 several compacts were signed with various other tribes. Today, eleven Wisconsin tribes operate casinos; all compacts expire between 2003-2004 (352).

Desiring to improve their economic well being, the Menominee began looking at the possibility of opening an off-reservation casino resort in Kenosha, Wisconsin. By the time the tribe started looking into the possibility, in 1997, the city had begun to fall on hard times. Manufacturing jobs, the base of its community, began to dissolve. Needless to say, the city welcomed the building of a resort casino.

The tribe chose what they considered to be a perfect location. Kenosha is located between Chicago and Milwaukee. The combined population of those two cities is over 11 million people (352). It only takes about 1 hour 20 minutes (66 miles) to drive from Chicago to Kenosha, and a little less than 1 hour (39 miles) from Milwaukee. According to tribal leader Apesanahkwat: "It's the most marketable location [for a casino] I've ever seen (Light & Rand 353).

The proposed placement of the complex, Dairyland Greyhound Park, would be expanded beyond its current status as a dog-racing track. In addition to the anticipated Class III gaming (3,600 slot machines, 120 blackjack tables, 200,000 square foot casino), the resort would also contain 3 hotels, a water park, a shopping mall, a convention center and a concert hall (351). Forecasts predicted 7.7 annual visitors, along with $514 million in revenues, and $243 million in profits (Pommer and Cole).

The impact on the surrounding area could be enormous. Total construction costs were estimated at $800 million, along with 3,500 new jobs (Light and Rand 354). Before any of this could be done, the tribe had to complete two objectives. First, the Bureau of Indian Affairs (BIA) had to place the land in trust; second, the governor had to agree and change the current compact.

The tribe was willing to make significant sacrifices for their new resort, "The Paradise Key." Aspects of tribal sovereignty would become nullified. For example, immunity would be waived in relation to violation of contracts. This would open the tribe to litigation. In addition, annual payments of $168 million would be made to the local government over a ten-year period (355). Reimbursement would be provided to the city, county and school district due to amplified public service needs (police, fire, sewer, water and emergency 911 system). Also, the Menominee agreed to pay the State at least $20 million in taxes, or 8% of the casino's net revenues whichever was larger; this money would be electronically transferred on a daily basis (356). Lastly, the tribe would swap one casino for another. The license on the Menominee's Crystal Palace, with 237 slot machines, would be exchanged for a license for the Paradise Key Resort.

The tribe's sacrifices might appear quite significant, but the Menominee would get some things in return. Paradise Key would be able to run blackjack tables 24 hours per day. Compacts with other tribal casinos only allow for 18 hours a day. In addition, the Menominee could offer roulette and craps. These two games are not available at other tribal casinos. Most importantly, the Menominee's new compact would open the door for other reservation casinos to make the same offerings! Wisconsin compacts allow for the negotiation of identical terms to those of other tribes. In other words, if Crystal Bay can offer blackjack for 24 hours a day, as well as roulette and craps, then other casinos could do the same. Basically, it appears the main importance, from an economic standpoint, is a superior location and a much larger casino.

The Menominee did obtain BIA approval; their only obstacle remaining was the governor's agreement to the compact. Although Governor Tommy Thompson appeared to favor the agreement, his appointment to President Bush's cabinet resulted in some issues for the tribe.

Lt. Governor Scott McCallum took Thompson's place. McCallum, in contrast to Thompson, did not approve of tribal gambling, especially the Paradise Key Resort. Governor McCallum "reiterated his resolve not to approve any new tribal casinos, whether on or off the reservation" (360). It now appears the Paradise Key Resort will not be built, at least not in the near future.

This new resort did not emerge, but new rules of politics could have been constructed. State governments might be more aggressive in their negotiations, especially when it comes to casinos off reservation land. For example:

- If local governments approve of tribal casinos, then Indians should also reciprocate by contributing needed funds for additional public services.
- States may insist on self-tribal nullification of aspects of their sovereignty: for example, full-regulation of gaming by the state and/or waiving immunity from lawsuits in gaming relating disputes.

An existing casino may be swapped for one that's proposed.

The happenings in Wisconsin also demonstrate the recent trends in politics concerning tribal/state compacts:

- More aggressive tribal attempts to build off reservation casinos.
- The emergence of mutually beneficial agreements between tribes and local governments in building off reservation casinos.
- A willingness on the tribe's part to share revenue with the state.
- A tribal willingness to give up certain aspects of their sovereignty.

If it appears the Wisconsin tribes had to jump through hoops in an effort to acquire off reservation land for a tribal casino, its nothing compared to the tribes in New Mexico. Their fight has involved a roller coaster ride of securing the right to place casinos on existing reservation land.

NEW MEXICO

Before the passage of IGRA, New Mexico allowed the following casino games to be operated by charitable organizations, as per the State's permissive lottery law: Twenty-One, Keno, Poker, Roulette and slot machines. Several charities operated video poker machines, even though these devices were illegal under New Mexico law.
The tribe of Sandia Pueblo began offering bingo in 1983 (Mason 87). After the passage of IGRA in 1988, Sandia Pueblo contacted the New Mexico Office of Indian Affairs and requested negotiations for a Class III gaming compact. The governor at the time, Garrey Carruthers, decided the tribe's request was a low priority item. Bruce King defeated Carruthers during the 1990 gubernatorial election. Accordingly, the issue fell in King's lap.

Some other tribes, Tesuque Pueblos and the Mescalero Apaches requested compact negotiation in May, 1991 (89). The Indians believed the New Mexico lottery law, allowing charitable organizations to operate LAS Vegas nights, would open the door for tribes to do the same. Certainly, the rulings of *Cabazon* and *Seminole*, along with the Pequot's fortune of teen casino nights, indicated full-fledged casinos would be operating in New Mexico. This case, however, proved to be somewhat different.

Negotiations between the state and two tribes (Sandia Pueblo and the Mescaleros) resulted in compacts in December of 1991 (89). Governor King, a Democrat, refused to sign these agreements. He stated: "I don't want to sign something New Mexicans don't want" (90). The Mescaleros, not wasting any time, filed a lawsuit against New Mexico in January 1992, for their failure to negotiate in good faith (90). The Sandia Pueblos filed a comparable lawsuit in July of that same year.

Much to the surprise of the tribes and the legal community, Federal District Court Judge John Conway rejected the tribe's arguments. Conway declared: "Congress [had] acted without authority in abrogating state 11th amendment sovereign immunity" (91). He came to this conclusion near the end of 1992.

Conway's ruling did not stop 10 tribes (the Jicarilla Apache, Mescalero Apache tribes, Pueblos of Acoma, Sandia, Pojoaque, San Juan, Toas, Isleta, Santa Ana, Tesuque) from flexing some muscle and offering various forms of gambling. In the meantime, King's unwillingness to negotiate compacts with the tribes tainted the historically good friendship between the Indians and the Democratic Party.

Those tribes involved in gambling, as a group, decided no political party could protect their economic well-being. They organized in November of 1993 and formed the "New Mexico Indian Gaming Association" (91). Their mission statement reads as follows:

> To protect and preserve the general welfare of tribes striving for self-sufficiency through gaming enterprises in Indian Country. To fulfill its mission, NMIGA works to develop sound policies and practices, provide technical assistance and advise on gaming related issues. In addition, NMIGA seeks to maintain and protect Indian sovereign governmental authority in Indian Country. (91)

By September 1994, the 10th Circuit Court of Appeals decided Conway's decision was incorrect. Basically, the appellate court decided the 10th and 11th Amendments did not protect the state from tribal lawsuits under IGRA. Soon thereafter, six tribes filed lawsuits against New Mexico, claiming, "the state had not negotiated in good faith" (100).

The decision of the appellate court and the tainted relationship between New Mexican Indians and the Democratic Party turned out to be a windfall for Republican governor primary winner, Gary Johnson. Indian governments involved with tribal gaming contributed $189,000 to Johnson's campaign (100). Mr. Johnson not only promised to sign Class III compacts, but also more importantly, "agreed to talk with [tribes], listen to [their] concerns on many issues, and respond to [them] openly and honestly" (101).

Governor Johnson declared on February 7, 1995, "that negotiations had produced an agreement acceptable to him and the tribes" (109). Eleven Indian nations and Governor Johnson signed the compact on February 13, 1995 (109).

Johnson declared the event a historic occurrence for New Mexico. He also reinforced the sovereign nature of New Mexico tribes by stating, "[The] compact is essentially a government to government agreement" (109). He also noted that without a compact between New Mexico and the tribal nations that, "the Federal government would force a compact on the state" (109). Johnson believed this would result in no state involvement with tribal gaming but more importantly, "No share in the revenues such games would generate" (110). The state/tribal compact allows:

> (1) Authorization for 'any and all Class III gaming'; (2) mechanisms for state review of tribal gaming records; (3) tribal regulations and audit procedures; (4) licensing requirements and background checks for casino employees; (5) standards for gaming equipment, supplies, and suppliers; (6) casino patron liability; and (7) criminal prosecutions under federal law. (110)

The tribes also saw it in their best interests to provide the state with the following yearly revenue amounts (per gaming facility):

- Three percent of the first $4 million of net win.
- Five percent of the net win over $4 million.

Sixty percent of the revenue amounts would go to the New Mexico State Treasury; forty percent to the local government.

More important for the tribes is the following agreement: revenue sharing with the state ceases "If the state permits any expansion of non-tribal Class III gaming in the State" (110). The above arrangement excluded State lottery, gaming operated by fraternal, veterans and non-profit organizations, and gaming machines operated by horse racing tracks. Even though Johnson significantly helped the Indians via good faith negotiating, and stood by the tribal nations, this did not stop the Indians from facing conflict.

The willingness of the tribes to organize and pool their resources (via NMIGA) helped them face the obstacles coming their way. The ability of the New Mexico tribes to organize their efforts is not a new phenomenon, but has occurred ever since 1598 (118). The All Indian Pueblo Council, Southern Governors Council, and the eight Northern Pueblos Council represent most of New Mexico's tribal pueblo members (118). Also, along with the support of two Apache tribes, the otherwise independent nations united to form "a loose collection of organizations that cooperate to accomplish a common objective" (118). The tribes used three tools to accomplish their economic/political goals regarding gambling: litigation, lobbying and electoral force.

<u>Lobbying Specifics: New Mexico Executive Branch</u>

The tribes lobbied primarily via contributions. Obviously, Governor King's interpretation of IGRA was quite different from the tribes' interpretation. King took a stance quite like that of President Andrew Jackson: Indians on reservations are located within a state. Therefore, they should be subject to laws just like every other citizen in the state. Rogin makes the preceding viewpoint clear in his book titled <u>Fathers and Children: Andrew Jackson and the Subjugation of the American Indian.</u>

While applying a strict state's rights approach, King used a somewhat famous strategy in trying to keep Indian casinos out of New Mexico. First, procrastinate and delay the compact negotiation process as long as possible. Second, when the tribes bring suit in Federal court, the state claims immunity under the 10th or 11th Amendment of the Constitution. Unfortunately for King, the tactic failed to work. Until Seminole Tribe of Florida v. Florida in 1996 the states were forced to negotiate compacts.

Lobbying Specifics: Legislatures

The New Mexico tribes took an assertive role within the State Legislature to form Indian gaming guidelines. NMIGA testified at New Mexico congressional hearings. New Mexico tribes also collaborated with the Federal Government on the "National Congress of American Indians/National Indian Gaming Association Task Force and Negotiating Team" (125). These organizations were created to smooth out differences between states and tribes.

Public Relations Electoral Pressure

Basically, the tribe's job in this arena was to convince the public that the benefits of Indian gaming outweighed the possible social costs. Tribes ran commercials and wrote articles for New Mexican newspapers. However, perhaps the most powerful PR tools were pre-addressed postcards sent to New Mexico legislators. As an example, the Isleta Gaming Palace urged guests to sign and send the following pre-stamped postcard to their respective state representatives/senators:

> I urge you to support Indian Gambling in New Mexico. I do! Indian Gaming provides well-run, legitimate entertainment for thousands of New Mexicans and visitors every day.
>
> Indian Gaming is a governmental enterprise supporting the tribes and surrounding area by creating jobs, new tax revenue and new business revenues within the state of New Mexico.
>
> I request that you support our Native American friends and oppose any effort that limits or reduces Indian Gaming. I will be supporting Indian Gaming With My Vote. (127)

Ready For Battle

The soap opera did not end after Johnson signed the compacts. Four months later, the New Mexico Supreme Court made a significant ruling in New Mexico ex. Rel Clark v. Johnson (N.M. Lexis; 904 p2d 11-1995). The Court found that Governor Johnson violated the State Constitution and performed a legislative duty by signing compacts with New Mexico tribes.

Basically, the New Mexico Supreme Court disagreed with Congress's passage of IGRA. They declared that IGRA gave, "State governor's power in excess that the governor possesses under state law" (Mason 149). Furthermore: "The Court prohibited 'all actions to enforce, implement, or enable any and all of the compacts and revenue sharing agreement'" (149). A couple of weeks after the ruling, the Court made an even stronger statement: "The compacts executed by the Governor are without legal effect and that no gaming compacts exist between the Tribes and Pueblos and the State of New Mexico. Thus New Mexico has not entered into any gaming compact that either the Governor or any other state officer may implement" (150). Obviously the New Mexico Supreme Court found the operation of casinos criminal in nature, not regulatory.

Of course, the tribes disagreed. The Secretary of the Interior in agreement with the provisions of IGRA had approved the compacts. Governor Johnson stood by the signed agreement and considered them valid. In addition, the tribes sent a letter to Johnson (along with a copy to the Albuquerque Journal on August 13, 1995) compelling him to stick by the negotiated compacts (152).

The State Supreme Court made another ruling on November 29, 1995 that raised the stakes even higher. They found the computer gambling game, "power bingo" to be an illegal slot under New Mexico law. Furthermore, the Supreme Court in the same ruling found charity Monte Carlo nights to be illegal (Citation Bingo LTD v. Otten, 1995 N.M. Lexis 426). In essence, this meant all gambling devices were found to be illegal, including those operated by fraternal organizations.

United States Attorney John Kelly after the *Citation* decision and in conformance with the New Mexico Supreme Court decision, requested the tribes to cease gaming operations on December 22, 1995. None of the casinos closed operations, and by January 3, 1996 the tribes filed a motion in Federal Court to stop the State from closing tribal casinos. The situation did become quite confrontational when Governor Viarrial of the Pojoaque Pueblo informed CNN: "We're prepared to die or go to prison in order to save that valuable way of making a living for our people" (Mason 156).

Things cooled down when both sides, the tribes and U.S. Attorney Kelly, agreed to allow Federal Court to determine the legality of New Mexico tribal casinos. The Indians agreed to close their doors if the Court decided, "that the tribal casinos are operating in violation of Federal law" (156). Some criticized Kelly, claiming he had given in to violent threats. He responded to those allegations and claimed he had defused a potentially dangerous situation.

Again, the sovereign nations decided it was in their best interest to pool resources and defend their ability to be self-sufficient. The Indians with a budget of $500,000 began a highly organized lobbying effort on three separate fronts. A never-ending battle occurred from the start to the finish of the 1996 legislative session.

(1) The tribes hired lobbying experts Rex Hockler and Odis Echols to work the State Legislature within the New Mexico Roundhouse.
(2) The tribes focused on Public Relations.
(3) The tribes continuously evaluated ongoing developments.

The tribe's efforts were to no avail. The legislature passed no bill allowing for tribal compacts. As of 1996, the only allowable gambling in New Mexico consisted of bingo, paper pull-tabs, pari-mutuel horse racing, pari-mutuel bicycle racing and a state lottery (163). The compacts were not worth the paper they were written on.

What Went Wrong?

Section 27103A of IGRA declares that the tribe must negotiate with the State for Class III gaming. However, IGRA fails to define "the State" (Mason 163). Mason recognized that "This ambiguity is a tacit recognition of federalism and the right of a state government to determine its constitutional and administrative procedures" (164).

This aspect of IGRA proved to be frustrating for the New Mexico tribes. At first, they issued their request for negotiation to the Office of Indian Affairs. Governor Carruthers then took over the process. After ousting King from office, Johnson came to an agreement with the tribes, only to be told that the compact was illegal. As already mentioned, the State Supreme Court decided only the Legislature can ratify Class III gaming compacts. It's interesting to note that the Legislature, under King, did pass a bill allowing the governor to negotiate gaming compacts; King vetoed it. Resisting the idea of providing a Republican governor with the same power, the house and the senate never considered a similar bill. Besides, the different opinions that existed between the left and the right resulted in nothing being accomplished. House Minority Whip Kip Nicely summed it up: "Really, the underlying theme of this whole session has been: Who is in charge of this place?" (164)

Current Status

The New Mexico Legislature, in 1997, finally passed a bill allowing legalized Indian casinos. Tribes were now allowed table games and slots. Regulation and control was left up to the sovereign governments, for the most part. Other stipulations included:

- Compacts to expire in nine years.
- The minimum age for gambling and employment set at 21.
- Aspects of Employment Law (leave, insurance, workers compensation, unemployment benefits, wages, allowable working hours) identical to those laws of New Mexico.
- Restrictions on check cashing.
- Prohibition of alcohol in gaming areas.
- Centralized auditing.
- Requirement of employee background checks

The issue, which brewed the most controversy, was the 16% tax required by the State (246). The state signed ten compacts on July 8, 1997. Secretary Babbitt noticed the high tax rate and made the following press release:

> On the one hand, they are expected to agree to a number of burdensome conditions that go well beyond the scope of any of the 161 compacts that are now approved between states and tribes in this country. On the other hand, if tribes do not agree to those conditions or if the compacts are disapproved, existing gaming establishments may be threatened with closure, causing immediate and enormous economic hardship. (246)

The tribes found the conditions so overwhelming that as of January 1, 1999, "Only the Pueblo gaming tribes have paid anything to the state" (246).

Most tribes remained reluctant to make payments to the state until threatened with a lawsuit. Finally, by November 2001, eleven tribes/pueblos agreed to a new compact. The agreement calls for the tribal nations to turn over $91 millions in back payments to the New Mexico treasury (Galilegos, *Court Fight* 2). However, the compact reduces slot machine payments in half to 8% (Gallegos, *Casino Deal* 1). This new arrangement will be up for renegotiation in 2015 (1).

Even though 11 tribes believed the new compact to be fair and reasonable, the Pojoaque Pueblo and Mescalero Apaches did not sign the agreement. The Pojoaques in an effort to assert their sovereignty "reject the idea" that slot machine profits should be shared with the state (Gailegos, Court Fight 1). The Denver Federal Appellate court will hear the case on January 16, 2002.

OREGON

Oregon did not follow New Mexico's lead. Agreeing with the rulings of *Seminole* and *Cabazon*, Oregon figured that if the State allowed any type of gaming for any reason, then it would be under an obligation to negotiate a tribal-state Class III compact.

Although the tribal-state negotiation process could provide for an interesting analysis, there is an issue of greater importance. Oregon is one of three states that allow a form of legalized sports wagering (Johnson 17).

Oregon has permitted pari-mutuel horse/dog racing since 1933. Also in 1971, the following games were excluded from the definition of illegal gambling: blackjack, roulette, and craps (9). However, certain restrictions applied to these games being operated in a legal manner. The games had to be played with tokens, not money. The tokens could only be traded for prizes. Another restriction: "State statute provides that charitable, fraternal, and religious organizations are the only entities permitted to profit from the operations of this type of contest" (9). The Oregon constitution was changed in 1976 to allow these same groups to operate bingo and raffles.

Additionally, "social games" became legal in 1974 (9). According to statute, a social game is defined as: "A game, other than a lottery between players where no house player, house bank or house odds exist and there is no house income from the operation of the social game" (Or. Rev. Stat. 167.117-20a). The statute also calls for each player to rotate the responsibility of dealer. Counties or cities have the authority to allow social games "in private businesses, private clubs, or places of public accommodation" (Johnson 9).

Since 1984, Oregon has been busy expanding gaming, via the state lottery, and has allowed the following games: scratch tickets, weekly drawings (since 1985); daily drawings, break opens (since 1987); sports action (since 1989); Keno (since 1991); video lottery, power ball (since 1992) (9).

Tribal-State Compacts/Oregon Gaming

As mentioned before, Oregon takes the position, according to its interpretation of IGRA that Tribal Nations must be allowed to operate all of the games mentioned above. Former Attorney General Theodore Kulongoski explains the state's competitive relationship with Indian tribes in Oregon:

> In combination with federal laws, Oregon's expansive gambling laws have created the opportunity for Federally recognized Indian tribes to offer casino gambling. Indirectly, then, state efforts to raise funds through casino-style games opened the door for expanded casino gambling by Oregon's tribes. The state has not only expanded gambling opportunities, it has created a competitive marketplace that increases pressure for each segment to become more ambitious in pursuit of revenues and market shares. (9)

Also, as a matter of public policy, Governor Kitzhaber "supports the principles of tribal economic self-sufficiency and respects the sovereignty of the tribal governments" (Gambling in Oregon 5). Kitzhaber also set forth the subsequent guidelines in relation to the development of Indian casinos:

(1) Kitzhaber believes and promotes that each Indian nation should have one gambling site per tribe.
(2) He also promotes, and took action via the Oregon State Police, to ensure the security of tribal-run games so they are conducted safely and honestly.
(3) Kitzhaber proposes and encourages charitable grants from Indian casinos. Hopefully, this action will build stronger ties between tribes and surrounding communities. (5)

At the same time, restrictions were also set on the growth of the State Lottery.

(1) Oregon should avoid expansion of Lottery gambling until the long-term social impact of gambling can be more accurately measured.
(2) The State should establish a research council charged with producing the necessary data for Oregon decision makers.
(3) Oregon law should be revised to reflect the changes in gambling, which have occurred in the last 25 years to attack illegal gambling. (1)

All of these measures allow the state of Oregon to analyze and evaluate the impact of gaming (both tribal sponsored and state sponsored) so that, "the maximum amount of net revenues to benefit the public purpose [in the Constitution], commensurate with the public good" (3-4).

Oregon tribes began the compact process in 1992 (Johnson 10). According to State law, either the governor or governor's delegates have the authority to negotiate a compact (Or Rev. Stat. 190.110-2). As of Spring 2001, the State has established nine compacts that cover "every Federally recognized tribe in Oregon" (Johnson 10). Due to the wide variety of legalized regulated gaming in Oregon, compacts cover the following games: "video lottery games of chance, keno, off track pari mutuel wagering, black jack, craps, roulette, poker, mini-baccarat, let-it-ride and big six wheel" (10)

<u>Sports Wagering</u>

Two tribes (Confederated tribes of Grande Ronde & Cow Creek Band of Umpqua) at the beginning of 1997 came to an agreement with the State to offer race and sports wagering on contests outside of Oregon if and only if "Oregon teams were not involved" (10).

The Bureau of Indian Affairs (BIA) approved the compacts, pending the Federal legality of the tribal-state agreement. The other tribes, awaiting the legal outcome, are ready to negotiate a similar compact.

Tribal gaming has been a long tradition in Oregon State. Sports betting has been a cultural part of tribal gambling since before the arrival of the first European settlers (Thompson 56). Wagers were placed on lacrosse and football like games, along with foot races, horse races, and events involving hunting and battle. Losses could be significant. Wives and family members could be lost, along with every "worldly good" owned. The

Indians considered their luck, whether good or bad, to be predetermined. Luck, according to Native Americans, occurs because of the Gods' intentions.

This, in itself, does not allow tribes to offer race and sports books. However, the Grand Ronde and Cow Creek figured if Oregon authorized sports betting via the State lottery and "the criminal code permits the activity by individuals who gamble for casual, non-profit purposes" then tribal members concluded Indians should be able to make the same offering (Johnson 18). The State agreed.

Just after the signing of the compacts, several sports organizations objected, especially the National Basketball Association. They believe the Professional and Amateur Sports Protection Act (PAPSA) bans the Oregon tribes from offering sports wagering. The conclusion was reached because PAPSA prohibits a state to "authorize sports betting of any kind" (U.S.C. 3702-1994). PAPSA does however include four exclusions to the rule. The law does not apply to the following exceptions:

(1) A lottery, sweepstakes, or other betting, gambling, or wagering scheme in operation in a State or other governmental entity, to the extent that the scheme was conducted by that State or other governmental entity, at any time during the period beginning January 1, 1976, and ending August 31, 1990;

(2) A lottery, sweepstakes, or other betting, gambling, or wagering scheme in operation in a State or other governmental entity where both

(a) such scheme was authorized by statute as in effect on October 2, 1991; and

(b) a scheme described in section 3702 (other than one based on pari-mutuel animal racing or jai-alai games) actually was conducted in that State or other governmental entity at any time during the period beginning September 1, 1989, and ending October 2, 1991, pursuant to the law of that State or other governmental entity;

(3) A betting, gambling, or wagering scheme, other than a lottery described in paragraph (1), conducted exclusively in casino located in a municipality, but only to the extent that

(a) such scheme or similar scheme was authorized, not later than one year after the effective date of this chapter, to be operated in that municipality; and

(b) any commercial casino gaming scheme was in operation in such municipality throughout the ten year period ending on such effective date pursuant to a comprehensive system of State regulation authorized by that State's constitution and applicable solely to such municipality; or

(4) Pari-mutuel animal racing or jai-alai games. (U.S.C.3704-1994)

Oregon has found itself in a no win situation. Refusing to negotiate the compacts could be seen as an act of bad faith. On the other hand, by signing the compacts, the

State could be violating Federal law. The only way to legally allow the tribes to offer sports betting is to find a loophole in one of the exceptions.

Exception #1 did not intend to stop Oregon or Delaware from offering sports betting via state lottery. It also allows tribal nations with appropriate compacts to continue offering sports wagering that were in existence before August 31, 1990, for example, off track wagering. It is the last sentence in Exception #1that prevents tribes from offering sports bookmaking because no Indian casino made this offering before August 31, 1990. Casinos were not in operation in Oregon between 1984 and 1993, therefore Exception #3 is not relevant. Dog/horse racing and jai alai are not the problem; therefore the Exception #4 is not pertinent. It seems the only saving grace for Oregon and the tribes rests with Exception #2.

Exception #2 appears to allow Nevada the ability to continue to permit sports wagering (Johnson 18). Sports books were legal in Nevada between September 1, 1989, and August 31, 1990. Also, a careful look at this exception reveals that professional/amateur sports wagering only had to be "conducted in that state" between September 1, 1989, and October 2, 1991 (PAPSA 3704-a-2).

The tribe could make the case that between the dates of September 1, 1989, and October 2, 1991, that Oregon allowed professional/amateur sports wagering "by individuals and organizations who gamble for casual, nonprofit purposes" (Johnson 15). For example, an office sports pool. The only stumbling block with this argument is that a court must agree this definition equals sports wagering.

If the case ever reached the Supreme Court, then they might be more willing to agree with the tribe's argument. The high court, in deciding McClanahan v. Arizona State Tax Commission, declared, "doubtful expressions are to be resolved in favor of the weak and defenseless people who are the wards of the nation, dependent upon its protection and good faith" (411 U.S. 164, 174-1973).

As of the writing of this thesis, the issue is at a standstill. Progress has not been made in establishing an Oregon Tribal Sports book. Neither has a court provided a decision on the matter.

Oregon's Similarity to Nevada

It must also be mentioned that Oregon, as a State, also shares some gaming characteristics with Nevada to the extent that Oregon citizens have access to a wide variety of forms of popular gaming. Oregon's eight tribal casinos, dog/horse racing, charity bingo, State lottery and 8,826 video poker machines allow the Oregon visitor/citizen a wide variety of options regarding gaming entertainment, much like that of Nevada.

NEVADA

Nevada has offered legalized gaming since 1931. The Silver State above all others could provide some insight into effective tribal gaming regulation for all states with Class III compacts.

Some claim Nevada possesses a tainted history when it comes to casino regulation. Books like The Green Felt Jungle (1963); House of Cards (1978) and Casino

(1995) point out the possible relationship between crime and Nevada gaming. Finally, the National Gambling Impact Study Commission issued a report in June of 1999. A "best practice" model is located within their testimony (NGISC 3-20). Nevada has already implemented most of the suggestions in that model, including such things as:

- Gambling statutes that provide a clear articulation of public purpose.
- A commitment to the overreaching principle of integrity.
- Administrative decision making placed in the hands of an appointed independent body.
- Independence in licensure decision- making.
- Burden of licensure suitability placed upon the applicant.
- Comprehensive disclosure of financial and political relationships.
- Requirements that ensure confidentiality in the treatment of sensitive personal and financial information balanced by appropriate public meeting requirements.
- A foundation of gaming regulation based on the assumption that those involved in the ownership or control of casino operations must be deemed 'suitable' for licensure or involvement in gambling.
- A regulatory body authorized to conduct in-depth background applicant/ employee background investigations. (3-20)

Nevada has negotiated three separate compacts with three tribal nations. Regulatory oversight with two of the compacts rests with the State, just like any non-tribal casino. The third compact covers a tribe, the Moapa Band of Paiute Indians, which only operates slot machines (Hill 46). There are also some other stipulations with this non-conventional compact: only tribal members can operate the casino; the total number of slots is limited, the slots must conform to State standards, the slot machines must also be purchased/sold through licensed businesses. The tribe in this compact maintains all enforcement duties. However, the Gaming Control Board (GCB) will, at the tribe's petition, "conduct random inspections of slot machines and provide other assistance at the request of the tribe" (52). The Nevada GCB has never experienced any problems with the Moapa casinos. Nevertheless, the compact calls for mediation/arbitration in the event of a violation of the tribal/State arrangement. If this results in a standoff, then the State has no option but to "seek an injunction directing closure of the gaming facility" (Hill 54). Also, any guest visiting this tribal casino is partially aware of the tribe's relationship with the State. Signs are posted in this casino that, in effect, declare, "[This gaming] facility is not licensed by the State [of Nevada]" (52).

Nevada Gaming Control organizational structure consists of three separate organizations, each performing a separate function. First, the Gaming Commission consists of five members, appointed by the governor. The Commission has the final say in all gaming matters. Second, the Gaming Control Board consists of three members, also appointed by the governor. The Board "is the regulatory, investigative, and enforcement branch of the system" (47). Within the GCB, five separate departments (Administration, Audit, Corporate Securities, Electronic Services, Enforcement, Investigations, and Tax/License) help ensure that gaming is conducted in a fair and honest manner. The Board also makes certain that correct State tax revenue is paid. In addition, the Board is responsible for keeping criminal elements out of the industry. The

Board also covers tribal oversight, licensing, monitoring and enforcement as requested by state-tribal compact. Thirdly, a nine associate Gaming Policy Committee is appointed by the governor to act as an advisory committee. The Committee makes policy suggestions to the Board and Commission.

<u>Funding</u>

According to the specifics of the compacts, tribes pay one of two figures to the GCB.

- One percent of gross gaming revenue or
- Costs incurred by the State for "Oversight/Regulatory Activities" (50).

It should be noted that non-gaming facilities are charged between 3 to 6.25 percent based on revenue amounts (50).

<u>Licensing</u>

Before an individual can be licensed, he/she must pay the entire investigation expense. Even if the potential licensee is denied, money will not be refunded. This holds true for a non-tribal member, and Indians in a tribe that Nevada licenses.

<u>Oversight</u>

The GCB regulates the Avi Casino (Fort Mojave Tribal Nation) and the Las Vegas Paiute Resort (Las Vegas Paiute Tribe) just like any other gaming operation in the State (46). Civil, criminal, licensing, and enforcement responsibility with these two tribes have been transferred to the State.

<u>Monitoring</u>

Regardless of the compact, the State stresses the importance of "independent accountant's reports of the gaming operation's financial statements" (52). This helps uncover any nefarious activities that might be occurring.

Again, two of the three tribes are treated just like any other gaming operation. These two tribes submit to undercover investigations, audits, stockholder monitoring and laboratory slot machine inspections.

<u>Enforcement</u>

These two tribes permit the State to inflict criminal sanctions for any violation. The State can temporarily stop casinos from operating or "revoke the license of [the] establishment or person" (53-54). Fines can also be levied between $25,000-$250,000 "for each separate violation of gaming regulations" (54).

<u>Essential Regulatory Elements According to Nevada's Gaming Control Board</u>

Nevada claims to use the most effective regulatory casino structure. This is very important to the State for two reasons. First, casino gambling is necessary to the State's economy. Second, the public must have no doubt that gaming is "conducted honestly and free from corruptive and criminal elements" (54). Due to these two reasons, the Nevada GCB believes that regulation has to be so strict that the public will never lose confidence in legalized casino gaming.

The GCB notes that, for regulation to be successful, the following standards must be followed:

(1) The regulatory body must maintain independence from the gaming industry.
(2) Adequate staffing must be provided to the regulatory body.
(3) Employees of the regulatory body must be permitted free access to any licensee's operation, 24 hours a day. This is vital to assure that proper procedures are being followed.
(4) Minimum Internal Control Standards must be state sponsored.
(5) Independent accountants must verify accounting records.
(6) Enforcement must have legal authority to discipline gaming licensees for non-compliance and serve as a neutral third party, when resolving guest disputes.

ARIZONA

An interesting argument occurred between Arizona and their tribal nations. These disagreements revolve around two critical issues: effective regulation and control. The ability to provide gaming entertainment with honesty and integrity depends on these two elements. As already mentioned, Nevada might have a superior regulatory structure. Compare and contrast the Nevada model with that of The Arizona Department of Gaming and the Arizona Tribal Gaming Regulators Alliance.

Arizona tribes were given the opportunity to reply to the accuracy of statements made by the Arizona Department of Gaming (ADOG) referring to what the tribes consider as unnecessary control asserted by the State. The tribes claim that the state of Arizona made several incorrect proclamations in the May 1998, General Accounting Office report, titled "Casino Gaming Regulation-Role of Five States and the National Indian Gaming Commission" (Hill).

This confrontation between states and tribal reservations is not unknown; it is almost a cliché. How does it often come to pass? Quite simply, the Federal Government considers tribes as domestic dependent sovereign nations. The decisions of numerous court cases, some of them previously mentioned, reaffirm the independent nature of tribal reservations.[2] Furthermore, many tribes contend that their relationship with the Federal Government is more important that their relationship with the state. This adds fuel to the often-fiery battle between state and tribe. The Federal Government, in fulfilling decisions made by the Supreme Court, often sides with the arguments of tribal nations.

Some states, although not all, on the other hand, argue the point made by former President Andrew Jackson. Tribal nations reside within a sovereign state of the United States. Therefore, these states reason they should have some control over what occurs on reservation land (Wallace, Rogin).

Arizona Department of Gaming

---

[2] The Supreme Court also declared in 1983 that: "The sovereignty retained by tribes includes the power of regulating their internal and social relations" (New Mexico v. Mescalero Apache Tribe, 462 U.S. 324, 332-1983).

The Arizona Department of Gaming (ADOG) was created in 1995, under the Arizona State Gaming Agency, to "carry out the State's responsibilities under the Indian Gaming Regulatory Act and the gaming compacts negotiated pursuant to the act" (31).

ADOG claims to monitor and enforce tribal gaming compliance as well as performing employee background checks. In addition, ADOG maintains they execute license certification, monitoring, and enforcement. In regard to enforcement, "the Tribal Affairs Investigations Unit is the primary unit charged with enforcing compact provisions at gaming facilities. This unit conducts background investigations on all key employees, primary management personnel, and casino employees submitting renewal applications" (33)

Licensing

Arizona tribes license non-Indian employees and managers. The tribes also license "manufacturers, suppliers of gaming equipment, distributors of gaming devices, and management contractors" (35). The state certifies employees or firms wishing to do business with the tribes. The certification for tribal members is for the most part just a recommendation.

Even if the State denies certification for a tribal member, the person can still work if a tribal forum overturns the State's recommendation. Nonetheless, compacts declare that casinos cannot hire anyone "convicted of any felony or gaming offense" (36). If an Arizona casino inadvertently hires anyone found guilty of the above offenses, they must be terminated immediately.

Monitoring

The tribes perform "regulation, control, and security" for their respective casinos (36). ADOG can, according to their claims, monitor tribal gaming to ensure compliance with the compacts. Furthermore, ADOG claims: "The Department has unrestricted access to public areas but generally must provide notice to enter nonpublic areas" (36). As mentioned previously, Nevada's GCB cites an independent regulatory body's free access as vital to ensure proper procedures are being followed.

ADOG can review financial records, but, at the same time, a tribe can review ADOG's "records on the tribe's casino gaming" (36).

Enforcement

ADOG claims shared responsibilities with tribal nations in regard to compact compliance. Also, the tribe looks into repeated compact violations and sends a report to the state. ADOG then does an independent investigation. If the issue cannot be resolved between the State and the tribe, then the matter can only be settled via filing suit through the Federal District Court.

ADOG cannot "assess fines/penalties, seize illegal equipment, or resolve patrons' disputes" (37). Nevada would not find this acceptable under their regulatory guidelines. According to the Nevada GCB, enforcement must have legal authority to discipline gaming licensees for non-compliance and serve as a neutral third party when resolving guest disputes.

Essential Regulatory Elements According to the Arizona Department of Gaming

Much like Nevada's guidelines, ADOG does note the need for three essential elements for effective gaming control:

(1) A truly independent regulatory body
(2) Licensing, reporting, and audit requirements, and
(3) Minimum levels for internal control. (38)

ADOG makes note of the need for independent control. This oversight "should not be composed of individuals who have an interest in the gaming industry" (38).

ADOG also stresses the importance of licensing: "A licensing component should be included for the independent regulatory body (meaning the ADOG) to conduct background/financial investigations of individuals employed in the industry and companies seeking to conduct business with gaming facilities" (38). In Nevada, the GCB performs this function.

Finally, ADOG believes minimum internal controls are necessary for the "handling and protection of assets" and fulfillment with internal controls (38). The Nevada GCB insists on State sponsored minimum internal control standards.

Arizona Tribal Gaming Regulators Alliance (ATGRA)

Much like those in New Mexico, Arizona tribes recognized the benefits of an organized effort and formed the Arizona Tribal Gaming Regulators Alliance in 1994. ATGRA's mission statement is as follows:

> [ATGRA will] promote a cooperative relationship among the regulators of tribal gaming enterprises and promote regulatory standards, methods of operation, and educational seminars in order to create consistent regulatory practices through the exchange of thoughts, information and ideas for the mutual benefit of the Arizona Tribes. (84)

ATGRA responded to the General Accounting Office report (RCED98-97) and asserted it is full of half-truths. Furthermore, ATGRA declared ADOG's misinformation equals nothing more than attempts to "attack the sovereignty of Arizona Tribes" (84). ATGRA claims the following actions by ADOG infringe on the sovereign nature of Arizona tribal nations:

- ADOG can only monitor regulation performed by tribal gaming commissions. However, ADOG tries to claim the role of co-regulator.
- ADOG continually increases staffing levels in an effort to increase their role to more than oversight.
- ADOG claims enforcement powers over Arizona Tribes. Tribes reiterate that ADOG can only monitor enforcement done by each tribal gaming office. In addition, ADOG has no investigative authority.
- ADOG has access to public areas, but must always provide notice to enter nonpublic areas.

- ADOG does not have dual responsibility for ensuring compliance with the Compact. The responsibility is only granted to the respective Tribal Gaming Office.
- ADOG does not conduct independent investigations of compact violations, but rather reviews the investigation done by the regulatory agency charged with the authority to investigate, the Tribal Gaming Commission. (84-87)

ATGRA agrees with the three regulatory guidelines ADOG submits on page 58. ATGRA, however, declares the National Indian Gaming Commission (NIGC) "performs these functions" (87). Also, independent accounting firms complete audits of each tribal gaming operation (according to stipulations in the compacts). The information in these audits is sent to the National Indian Gaming Commission.

ATGRA, in conclusion, reiterates its determination to provide strong gaming regulation. ATGRA also believes its "licensing component is more stringent, in most cases, than the licensing done by the [Arizona] Department [of Gaming]" (87). ATGRA would also prefer "an increased role in Class III gaming by the National Indian Gaming Commission" (87). ATGRA finishes by saying:

> The NIGC has shown the ability to objectively monitor gaming on sovereign lands while the Arizona Department of Gaming has constantly attempted to limit and reduce gaming done on Tribal Sovereign Lands. And this is not their role as defined by IGRA or the Compact. (87)

Basically, the Arizona tribal nations do their best to limit the State's authority to regulate gaming on reservation land. The two groups argue instead of cooperate. California state and tribal nations might want to mimic Nevada's regulatory model. This could result in less red tape, therefore allowing California tribal gaming to realize its full potential. In turn, Nevada casino operations, especially in Reno/Sparks, should carefully monitor the happenings in California. Smooth, mutually beneficial agreements that occur between the State and California tribes could result in tribal casinos opening faster than expected. Power struggles, and arguments over sovereignty might result in nothing being accomplished, therefore giving Reno/Sparks casino operations more time to develop an economic defense strategy.

WASHINGTON

Washington State takes a different approach to tribal/state interaction in contrast to the apparent adversarial relationship between the Arizona Department of Gaming and the Arizona Tribal Gaming Regulators Alliance. Washington and compacted tribal nations[3] maintain and build a positive and cooperative partnership (79). The State deals "with tribes on a government to government basis while balancing the State's duty to the public" (79). Also, State Agents assigned to the Washington State Gambling

---

[3] Washington State held compacts with the following tribal nations as of late 1998/early 1999: Swinomish Indian Tribal Community, Jamestown S'Klallam Tribe of Washington, Suqamish Tribe, Squaxin Island ndian Tribe, Confederated Tribes of the Chehalis Reservation, Nisqually Indian Tribe, Puyallup Tribe of Indians, Muckleshoot Indian Tribe, Tulalip Tribes of Washington, Upper Skagit Indian Tribe and Nooksack Indian Tribe of Washington.

Commission's Tribal Gaming Unit must finish training classes that provide broad familiarity on Indian anthropology/culture. This training is specific to the Agents' assigned reservation casino.

Compact Construction

According to the tribal-state compact, the State restricts the number of casinos, betting limits and operational hours. If the State is satisfied with tribal regulation and control occurring within the tribal gaming operation, then authorization will be provided to expand the casino. The procedure is illustrated in the following example: "Tribes may operate up to 31 gaming tables and allow wagers up to $250 during the first six months after which these may be increased to 52 tables and wagers up to $500" (76-77).

Any disputes that arise between the State and the tribe in regard to compact interpretation are settled through negotiation, arbitration and even possibly, injunction (79). Nonetheless, regulatory and control duties are truly shared between the tribe and the State. The shared responsibilities will be described in the following categories.

Oversight

One example of shared responsibility is oversight. Administration primarily resides with individual Tribal Gaming Agencies. The State, however, assists the tribes with license certification, monitoring, and enforcement.

Licensing

The State and the tribe share in the task of approving licenses for "gaming employees, management companies, manufacturers and suppliers of gaming services and those extending financing of the gaming operation" (77). But the State does take the "final responsibility for approving an applicant" (77). The tribe might perform a background investigation, but the State always does so as a matter of policy.

Monitoring

Again, the tribal casino and the State share responsibilities in the area of monitoring gaming operations, thus helping to guarantee agreements set forth in the compact. Tribal Gaming Agencies perform regulation, Control and Security (77). The state then does independent screening of the tribal casino to ensure compact compliance. Much like Nevada's GCB agents, Washington's agents have "unrestricted access" to public and non-public areas (78). Undercover agents could perform this State monitoring or Washington Gaming Control might announce their visit to a tribal casino (78).

Enforcement

The State and the tribe have "similar enforcement authorities" (78). The tribal nation "has primary responsibility for [compact] enforcement (78). However, much like Nevada, Washington Gaming Control Agents serve as an independent enforcement body. State enforcement Agents has the legal authority to discipline gaming licensees for non-compliance via monetary fines. Interestingly enough, any fines collected goes to "nonprofit organizations" instead of going into the State treasury (78).

Essential Regulatory Elements According to the Washington State Gaming Commission

Washington State believes compacts written with tribal nations should accomplish two goals:

(1) The interests of both the State and the tribe are achieved.

(2) Rules should always be established so that "the integrity of gaming is beyond reproach" (79).

According to the State of Washington, these goals will be partially achieved through "comprehensive background investigations" and "independent verification" of games to ensure they are "operated fairly" (79).

In summary, according to the Washington Department of Gaming, the tribes and the State stand on equal ground. According to Washington State, this attitude allows for both parties to create a mutually beneficial agreement. In addition, this also helps "to maintain and build a positive and cooperative partnership" (79). Washington hopes this tactic will allow for "voluntary [tribal] compliance" (79). A "heavy-handed [state] approach" then becomes un-necessary (79).

Extraction of General Patterns/Lessons from the above Examples

- Even though ADOG and ATGRA claim they both desire effective regulation and control, both sides are divided on how to achieve these two objectives. Working together, instead of taking part in a power/sovereignty struggle might be more productive.

- Cooperation, instead of conflict, might result in more productive regulation.

- An excellent example of the state and tribe working together is found in the Nevada tribal/state relations. Although, the Las Vegas Paiute Tribe, and the Fort Mojave Tribal Nation basically conform to state regulations already in place, the Moapa Band of Paiutes essentially undertake all enforcement duties. The compact does contain numerous checks and balances. Only tribal members can operate the casino, slots (the only game allowed) must conform to state standards. In addition, the Nevada Gaming Control Board will conduct inspections of the slots and offer other assistance at the tribe's request. If the State believes the tribe is not living up to the agreements in the compact, the issue can be settled through arbitration and mediation.

- Checks and Balances can also be found in Oregon's tribal/state agreement. If the State is satisfied with tribal regulation and control, then permission will be granted to expand games and betting limits. In addition, regulation and control duties (oversight, licensing, monitoring, enforcement) are shared between the state and tribal nations. Overall, the two entities respect each other. It appears this leads to harmony between the state and tribe

- The same attitudes of respect found in Oregon are realized between Washington State and its tribal nations.

- Outright tribal gifts, for example, campaign contributions in New Mexico and revenue sharing in Connecticut, can help states/politicians realize the potential benefits of tribal gaming.

- With the Seminole decision of 1996, it might be in the tribe's interest to offer gifts to the state in which they reside to entice state governments to sign compacts. Also, it might be in the state's interests to insist on joint collaboration of enforcement duties.

- Local governments might be able to take advantage of tribal desires to establish a casino off reservation, as seen in Wisconsin. However, additional concessions might also need to be made to the state.

TRIBAL SUCCESS?

Looking at tribal success stories, such as the Pequot's Foxwoods in Connecticut, many people believe IGRA has proved successful in pulling a majority of Native Americans out of their desperate financial situation. This is clearly an incorrect statement. It has helped some tribes substantially, others moderately.

However, the great majority of Native Americans have received very little or no benefit from tribal gaming. Nonetheless, during a short ten-year period (from 1990 to 2000), "Wisconsin's Native American population on reservations and tribal trust lands increased by nearly 92%" (Light and Rand 352). This is an indication that more money can be made on reservation via tribal casinos than working off reservation.

Some Indian casinos have been so successful that casino ventures have become known as: "The new buffalo" meaning, casino gaming has become a successful method of sustaining life (Meyer and Hartman 53). Nettie Kingsley, Ho-Chuck tribal researcher for cultural preservation, declares: "More and more people are coming back to their homelands [. . .] because of the gaming. We don't need to go to the cities to work in the factories anymore. We found the golden egg, finally" (Light and Rand 352).

Sometimes non-tribal local government leaders see tribal gaming as a solution to the financial woes facing a city. Tom Ryan, Council President, Beloit City, Wisconsin, states, "Tribal gaming has pulled [the tribes] out of poverty, and it'll help pull [Kenosha, Wisconsin] out of poverty" (363). As already noted, the city of Bridgeport, Connecticut, hoped a casino would lessen their economic dependence on the defense industry.

A glance at some figures, however, paints a different picture. The May 1997 General Accounting Office (GAO) report titled, "Tax Policy-A profile of the Indian Gaming Industry" shows that a majority of the revenue/profit was earned by a small number of tribes. A 1995 analysis of sixty-six Class II gaming facilities shows more than half of the revenue/profit went to only eight tribes. That is to say, a minority of the tribes received the most money. See the figures below.

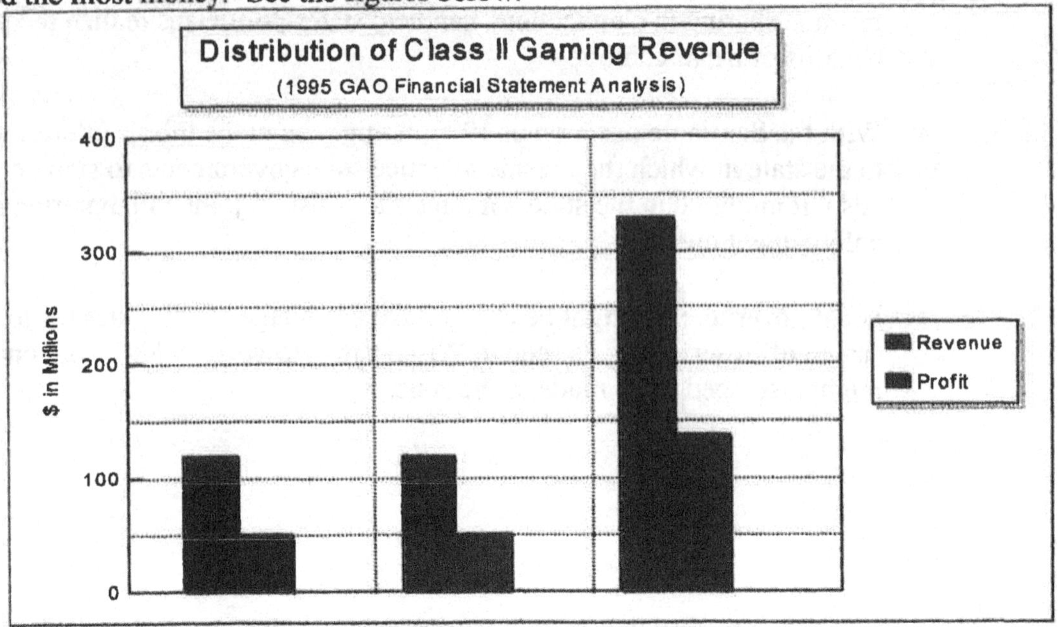

Source: General Accounting Office (GAO/GGD-97-91)

# of Tribes:	50	8	8
Revenue ($M)	<$10M	$10M to $20M	>$20M

These figures broken down into profit distributed per tribe are even more striking.

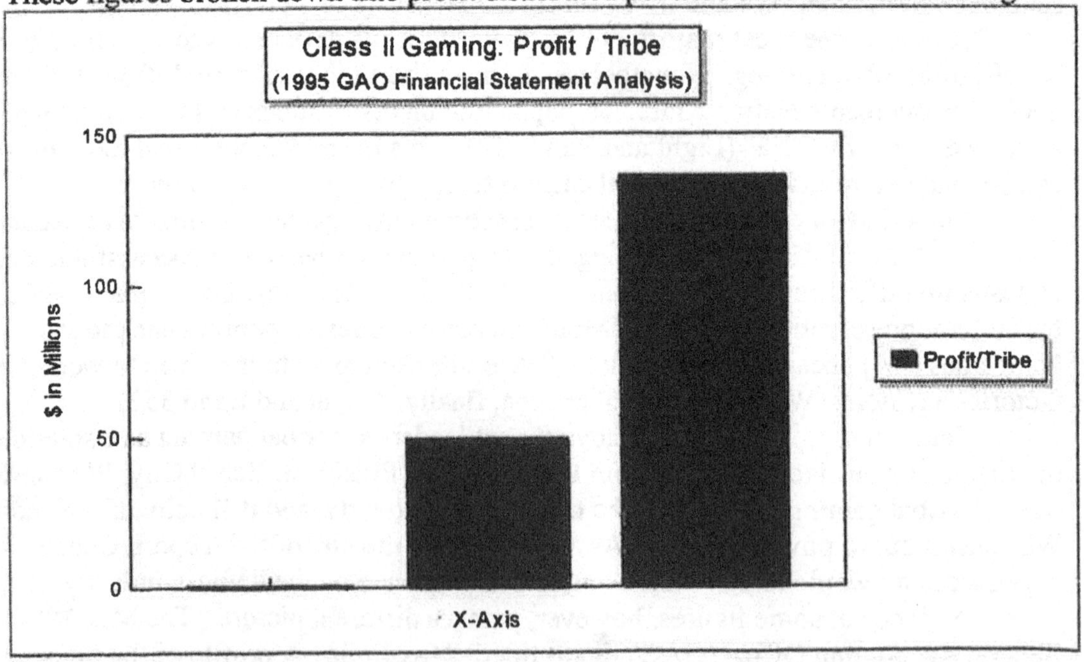

Source: General Accounting Office (GAO/GGD-97-91)

# of Tribes:	50	8	8
Profit/Tribe ($M)	$.9931	$6.19	$17.06

Likewise, the distribution of 1995 Class III gaming revenue provides similar results.

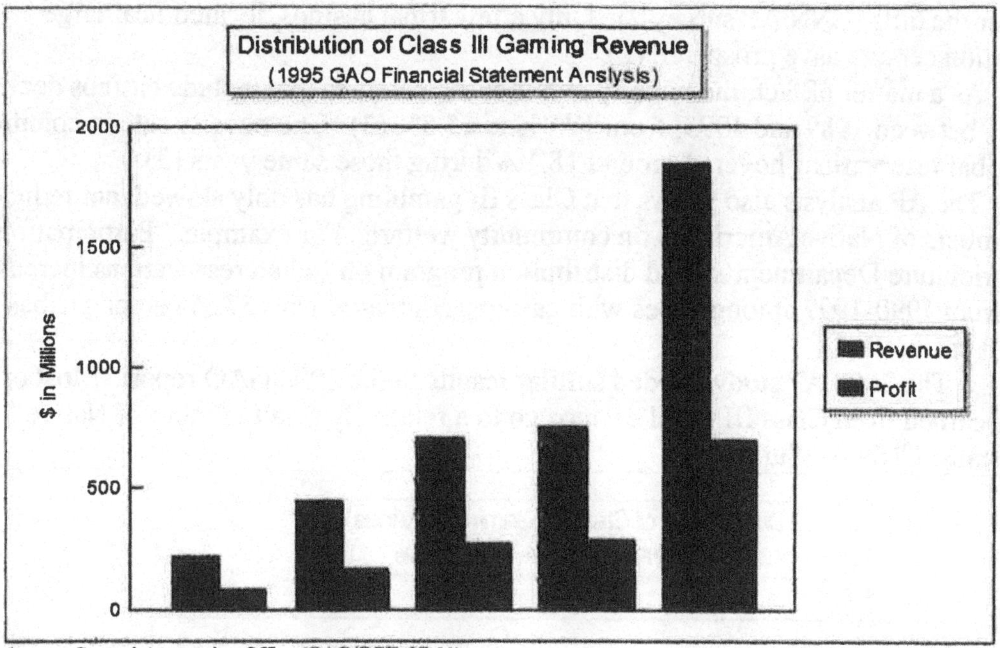

Source: General Accounting Office (GAO/GGD-97-91)

# of tribes	41	32	21	10	8
Revenue ($M)	<$10M	10$M to $20	$20M to $50M	$50M to $100M	>$100M

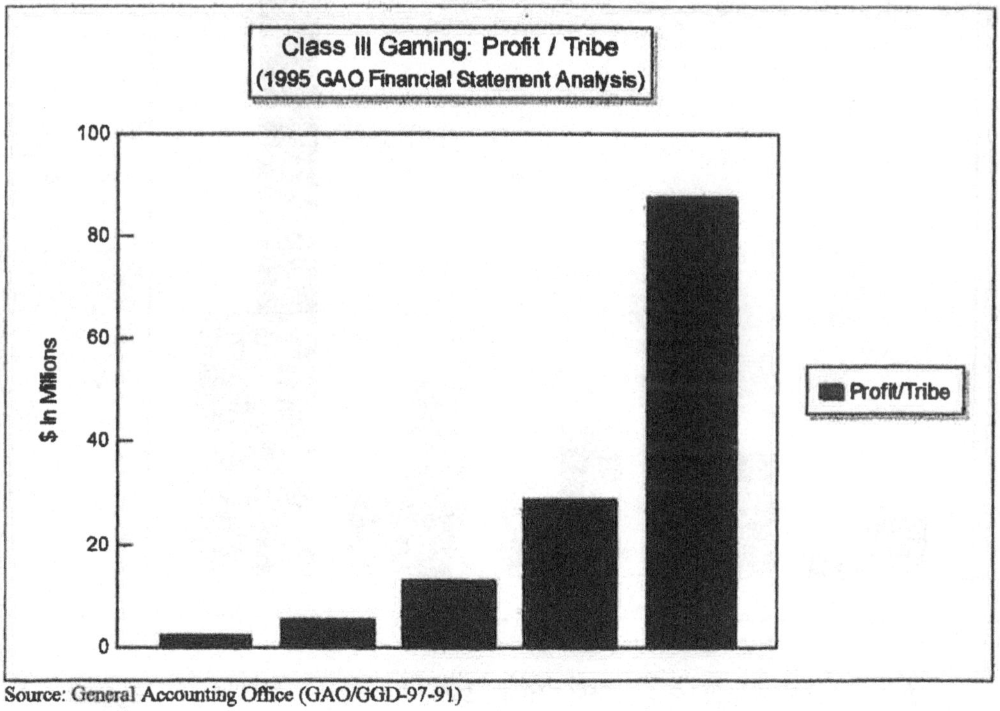

Source: General Accounting Office (GAO/GGD-97-91)

# of tribes	41	32	21	10	8
Profit/Tribe($M)	$2.01M	$5.32M	$12.85M	$28.69M	$87.83M

According to an August, 2000, study by Associated Press (AP), out of the 130 tribal casinos with Class III gaming, most tribes break even, making just enough money to cover the bills (CNN AP survey 2). Only a few tribal casinos, located near large population centers have prospered (2).

As a matter of fact, the poverty rate in those counties that include casinos declined slightly between 1989 and 1995, from 17.7% to 15.5% (3). The poverty rate in counties with tribal reservations hovered around 18.1% during those same years (3).

The AP analysis also shows that Class III gambling has only slowed, not reduced, the numbers of Native Americans on community welfare. For example, "Participation in the Agriculture Department's food distribution program on Indian reservations increased 8.2% from 1990-1997 among tribes with casinos, compared with 57.3% among tribes without casinos" (3).

The 2000 AP study yielded similar results to the 1995 GAO report. Most of the profits earned from Class III tribal casinos go to a relatively small number of Native Americans (CNN AP Survey).

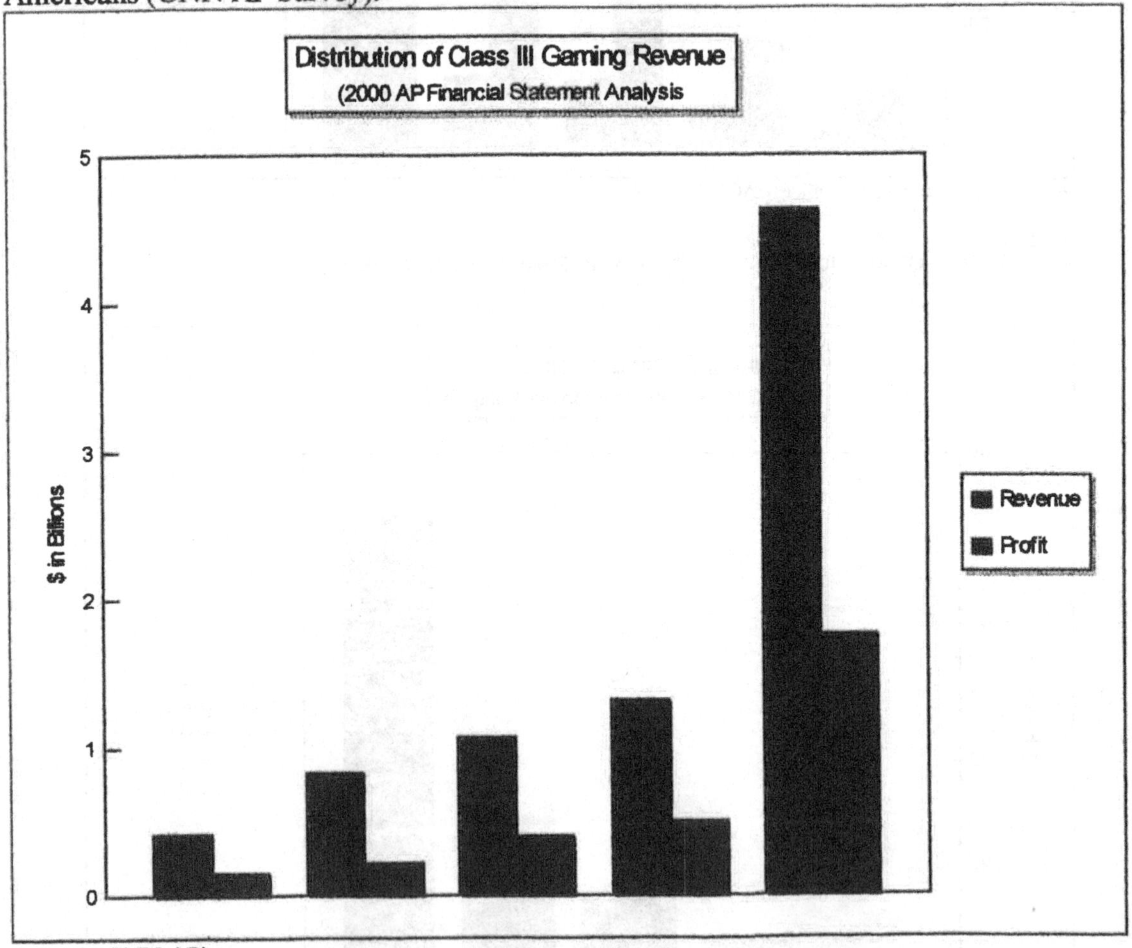

(Source: CNN AP)

Category	<$10M	$10M-$25M	$25M-$50M	$50M-$100M	>$100M
Total Revenue: (in $B)	$.413B	$.826B	$1.07B	$1.32B	$4.63B
Profit (in $B):	$.157B	$.214B	$.407B	$.502B	$1.76B
Approx. # of Tribal Members	253,000	95,000	38,500	30,500	80,000

For most Indians, the average profit per tribal member is miniscule. See the following graph.

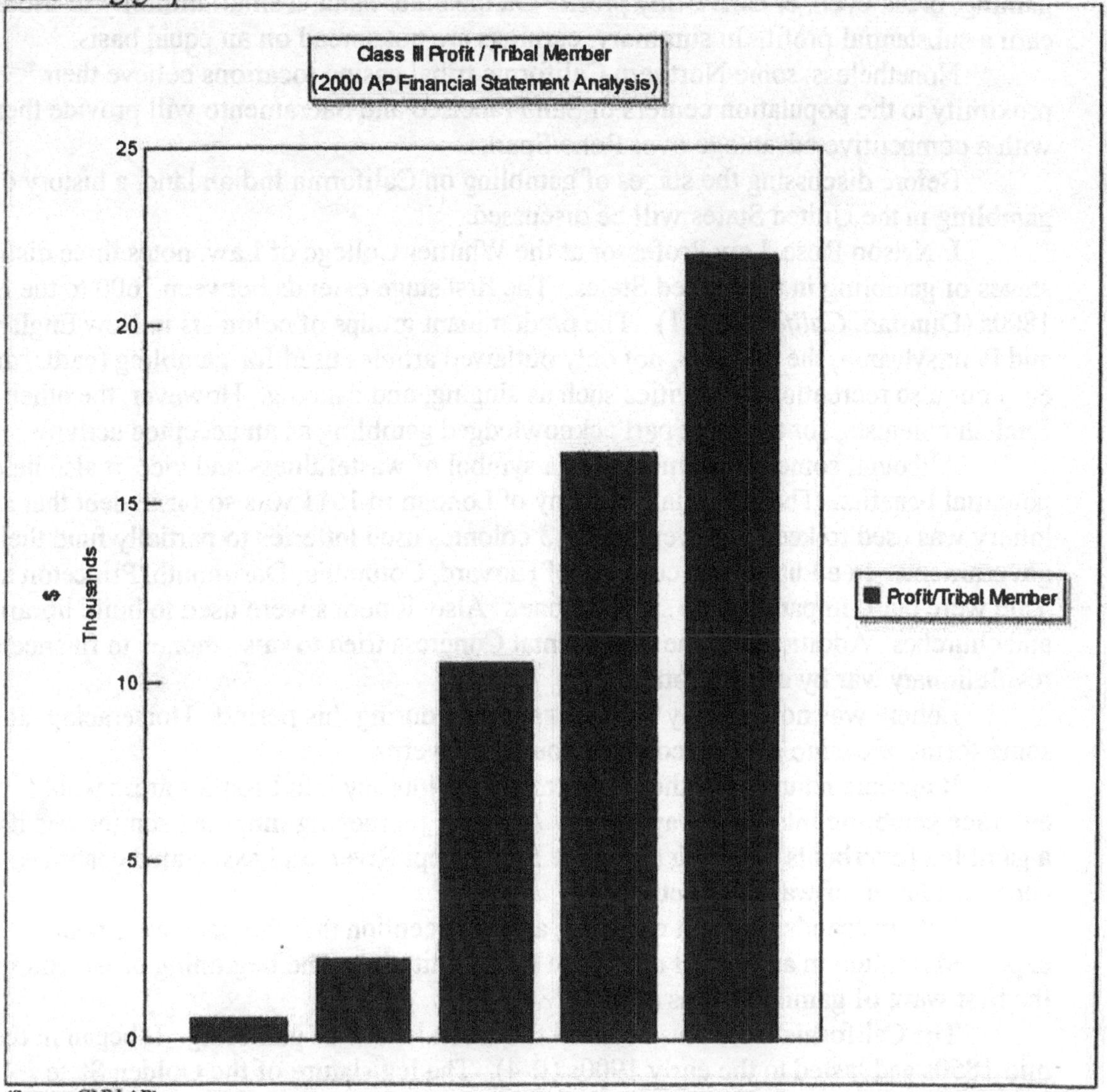

(Source: CNN AP)

Category	<$10M	$10M-$25M	$25M-$50M	$50M-$100M	>$100M
Approx. # of Tribal Members	253,000	95,000	38,500	30,500	80,000
Average Profit / Tribal Member	$620	$2,251	$10,561	$16,445	$21,992

According to the above figures, most tribal members, when it comes to Indian gaming, break even, or earn a tiny profit. On the other hand, a small minority of tribes earn a substantial profit. In summary, earnings are not spread on an equal basis.

Nonetheless, some Northern California tribal casino locations believe their proximity to the population centers of San Francisco and Sacramento will provide them with a competitive advantage over Reno/Sparks.

Before discussing the stages of gambling on California Indian land, a history of gambling in the United States will be discussed.

I. Nelson Rose, Law Professor at the Whittier College of Law, notes three distinct stages of gambling in the United States. The first stage extends between 1600 to the Mid 1800s (Dunstan, *California* II-1). The predominant groups of colonists in New England and Pennsylvania, the Puritans, not only outlawed articles used for gambling (cards, dice, etc.) but also recreational activities such as singing, and dancing. However, the other English colonists, for the most part acknowledged gambling as an accepted activity.

Although some saw gambling as a symbol of wastefulness and vice, it also held potential benefits. The Virginia Company of London in 1611 was so far in debt that a lottery was used to keep it solvent. All 13 colonies used lotteries to partially fund their governments. In addition, the colleges of Harvard, Columbia, Dartmouth, Princeton and Yale were built, in part, by the same manner. Also, lotteries were used to build libraries, and churches. Additionally, the Continental Congress tried to raise money to finance the revolutionary war by using a lottery.

Lottery was not the only form of gambling during this period. Horseracing, and some forms of casino gaming could be found in taverns.

It appears natural that those who made the journey into Frontier areas would embrace gambling into their way of life. After all, journeying into the Frontier was itself a gamble. Riverboats traveling along the Mississippi River, and associated channels, became a haven of wagering activity.

Lottery scandal, blatant cheating, and a perception that the poor were being exploited resulted in an overall change in moral attitudes. The beginning of the end for the first wave of gaming begins around 1800.

The California Gold Rush started the second wave of gambling. It began in the mid 1850s and lasted to the early 1900s (II-4). The legislature of the Golden State quickly outlawed banking games (where players placed wagers against the house) in an effort to reduce the social costs. Outlawing the games, however, did not stop gamblers from gambling, but only moved the green felt tables underground.

Some states in the South did use a lottery to help rebuild their prior Confederate states. Lotteries, for the most part, were privately run. To some extent for this reason, severe scandal swept throughout the gambling business. This put an end to this industry, once more.

Nevada's 1931 response to the Great Depression was the legalization of casino games. That started the third wave of gambling. The gambling industry started to move beyond Nevada in 1963 when New Hampshire legalized a state lottery. Atlantic City, New Jersey began offering casino games in 1978 (Eisler 97). IGRA opened the door for tribal gambling. Iowa started the trend in riverboat gaming in 1991. Casinos, including those run by tribal governments, can now be found in over 27 states.

GAMBLING IN CALIFORNIA

Before Proposition 1A

Before the passage of Proposition 1A (the measure that authorized Class III tribal gambling in California) gaming entertainment in the state consisted of state lottery, horseracing, card clubs, charity bingo, and different games played in Indian casinos. However, these tribal games had a questionable legal status. Just before Nevada-style gaming was authorized there, California was the 6th largest state when it came to money wagered (Dunstan, *California* V-1).

It should be mentioned that the state lottery was by far the most popular California game, with 59% of 1995 residents taking part in lotto (V-2). But when it came to casino entertainment, Californians, in that same year, made 14 million casino visits (V-2). California, as a state, ranks number one in providing gaming revenue to Nevada (V-2). California citizens, for the longest time, appeared content in traveling to Nevada to take part in casino gambling, while at the same time keeping a legalized vice out of their state. California has made attempts, after Nevada legalized casinos, to bring gambling in one form or another to their state. Most of these efforts failed. For example, greyhound racing was defeated in 1946 and 1976 (Dunstan, *Evolution* 373). A bill to allow casinos was shot down in 1950, and lotteries were disregarded in 1950 and 1964 (373).

However, some forms of gaming entertainment found their way into the state. Non-banking card games, such as poker, have been legal since 1849; pari-mutuel horse racing, since 1933; charity bingo, from 1976; and state lottery, from 1984 (373).

Card Clubs

Before Proposition 1A, the California Constitution never authorized a form of gambling; it just made prohibitions against what games could be offered. Card rooms were never prohibited. Therefore, they have been allowed since California has been a state. The average wager per person in 1995 was higher for California than any other state that allows card rooms. See the table below.

State	Per Capita Wagered
California	$283.10
Montana	$130.80
Washington	$43.10
Maryland	$39.10
North Dakota	$00.47

(Source: Dunstan, *Gambling in California* V-6)

The State in the past has viewed card rooms differently than full-fledged casinos for a couple of reasons.

- Players pay to take part in the game with others. The club, itself, does not benefit, based on the amount of money wagered.
- California card rooms have been able to offer so-called "Asian games" (pai gow poker, sic bo) that are very popular with the large Asian American citizens in California.

- A casino is designed, through mathematics, to separate cash from the customer. Playing cards against an opponent involves a high degree of skill; the money is basically redistributed among the different players. Nonetheless, it is estimated that card clubs generated revenue of $711 million in 1995 (V-7).

Card clubs can represent a significant source of a city's tax revenue. For example, the cities of Commerce, Bell Gardens, and San Pablo respectively have obtained 36.7% ($13.5 million), 44.3% ($8.9 million) and 45.7% ($3.7 million) of their budget from card club taxes (V-11).

Pari-Mutuel Horse Wagering

Even though horseracing has been legal since 1933, its popularity has been decreasing. For example, wagering on horses decreased from $4.68 billion in 1985 to $2.48 billion in 1995 (V 1-4). This is a 47 percent decrease (V-4). Furthermore, license fee revenue has decreased 27% from 1990 to 1995 (V-4).

Charity Bingo

This seemingly insignificant form of entertainment became a part of the catalyst that took the Cabazon's battle to the Supreme Court, and led to the passage of the Indian Gaming Regulatory Act. In 1995, low stakes charity, non-tribal bingo made up only about 2% of the overall gaming gross revenues within the state (V-14).

State Lottery

California jumped on the lottery bandwagon in 1984 (V-4). This was the second chance California had to authorize a lottery. The first initiative appeared in 1964. It's expected the measure lost because it called for a private firm, not the state, to run the game. Apparently, the public did not approve of a lottery monopoly placed in the hands of a private corporation.

Rodger Dunstan, Assistant Director of the California Research Bureau, like Nelson Rose, points out three waves of tribal gaming in California.

FIRST WAVE

Some California tribes began offering bingo and card games in the early 1980s. California, believing these were criminal acts, tried to shut down these tribal operations. As discussed previously, it was assumed Public Law 280 allowed the state to do this.

The Supreme Court's ruling of *Cabazon* stated otherwise. Tribes, under Federal law, can offer gaming if it's allowed in the state where the Indians reside. Generally speaking, the reason why the state offers gambling is of no consequence (as evidenced by Foxwood's offering blackjack, craps, roulette and poker based on the Connecticut law allowing post prom casino nights for high school kids).

It is the public policy of California to offer non-banking card games, bingo, and lottery. Since it is the procedure to allow these games, they are not criminal in nature. Therefore, the state cannot impose its rules and regulation on the tribes. In other words:

> The [Supreme] Court upheld, by a six to three vote, the right under federal law for Indians to offer gambling on reservations without state regulation in states where such gaming was legal for at least some non-Indian purposes.

> Since California had legalized card games, bingo, and lottery, the action against the tribes was not properly a criminal enforcement matter, but a civil action for which the sovereignty of tribes had left them largely immune to the actions of the state. (Dunstan, *Evolution* 373)

SECOND WAVE

The passage of IGRA set off the second wave of tribal gambling in California. Class III gambling (especially slot machines) began taking a place on reservations, without state-tribal compacts. Negotiations began, but fell through when California insisted that slots are illegal under the law. The tribes and the state decided to allow the Federal court to come to a conclusion regarding the slot's legitimacy.

While the battle waged in court, the San Diego police, in 1991, invaded three tribal gambling halls that operated slots. This raid was found to be unlawful. Even though the state proved its case (Rumsey Band of Wintun Indians v. Wilson) and slots were found to be illegal gaming devices, some tribes still offered them to guests. The Indians continued to appeal the Rumsey decision. Finally, the legal petitions for reconsideration were exhausted. However, by this time, 12,000 highly profitable slot machines were in operation in different reservation casinos.

The obvious disregard for the law appears to have backfired on the tribes operating one-armed bandits. Due to this reason, suppliers, gambling management companies, or financing firms refused to work with these tribes.

The sticking point of negotiations turned out to be the operation of slot machines. Casino operators know that this gambling device brings in the highest amount of profit. Governor Pete Wilson began Class III negotiations with the Pala Band of Mission Indians during December 1996 (Dunstan, *Evolution* 374). The Pala were chosen because they did not operate a casino, and therefore, could not be in violation of the law. It was expected negotiations with this band would be used as a model for other tribes.

The State and the tribe came to an agreement and formed a compact on March 6, 1998 (375). It consisted of the tribe offering a slot that actually classified as a vending machine. This was done to conform to the laws surrounding the State lottery. A vending machine would not be considered a slot machine under the California penal code. These gaming machines replicated the fundamentals of California's lottery game.

The idea of the Pala agreement becoming the model compact became moot after Proposition 5 passed in November of 1998 (375). The combined efforts of the California tribes placed this initiative on the ballot, and became accepted by the voters on a 2 to 1 margin (376). Proposition 5 would have allowed for Indian gaming devices, blackjack based on the concept of a player's prize pool, "any lottery game, including but not limited to drawings, raffles, match games, instant lottery ticket games" and off track pari-mutuel horse wagering (Hotel Employees & Restaurant Employees International Union v Gray Davis). However, Prop 5 was found to run contrary to the California State Constitution (Hotel Employees & Restaurant Employees International Union v Gray Davis). Not only would Prop 5 have allowed banking card games, but also "casinos of the type currently operating in Nevada and New Jersey" (Hotel Employees & Restaurant Employees International Union v Gray Davis). These activities were illegal in California at that time.

If you cannot beat them, join them. The tribes and Governor Davis, along with legislative approval placed Proposition 1A on the March, 2000 ballot. This would change the State Constitution, but, most importantly, open the door for slot machines on reservation casinos. The law passed, and the expected number of slot machines is estimated to be between 43,000 and 113,000 (Dunstan, *Evolution* 376). Ambiguities in the actual number of slot machines allowed occur due to compact interpretation. Some estimate the maximum number at 114,000 (Ader, Falcone and Adam Steinberg 9). Needless to say, the actual number of slot machines to be allowed in the state is the subject of much controversy. The controversy arises because the compact calls for a maximum of 44,000 tribal slot machines, but each tribe is allowed a maximum of 2000 slots. There are 57 tribes that signed Class III compacts with the State of California (9).

THIRD WAVE

The change in the State Constitution, and tribal success with the voters marks the 3rd wave of California Indian gaming. Please note the number of slots on reservations (table below).

YEAR	NUNBER OF SLOTS
1994:	4,780
1996:	12,100
1997:	19,078
2000:	22,859
2001:	25,196
2002:	40,883

Sources: Dunstan, *Gambling in California*
Yamamura

This third wave of California gambling could be interrupted if the California Card Clubs have their way.

Four San Francisco card clubs on November 17, 2001 in Federal Court argued that proposition 1A violates the 5th and 14th amendments of the U.S. Constitution because Native Americans in California and only Native Americans in that State can operate slot machines.

The card clubs do not deny that IGRA authorizes tribes to operate gambling, but the clubs argue only if that form of gaming is already allowed elsewhere in the State. Slot machines in California were illegal prior to 1A's passage. To put it another way, the clubs contend that after the change in the State Constitution, a specific group (the Indians) is provided with preferential treatment. This treatment, the clubs argue, is "a classification grounded on race or ethnic origin" and this violates the "Constitutional guarantee of equal protection"(Morain 2).

It should be kept in mind; the tribes are not being sued. The clubs are only making a request to the Federal Government: overturn Proposition 1A. On the other hand, the tribes want to intercede, believing that neither the State nor Federal Government can look out for Indian interests.

Tribal attorneys are requesting the case be thrown out of court, because the tribes cannot be sued (due to their sovereign nature), and any Federal ruling would have a direct impact on the Indian Nations. The tribes also argue that IGRA "permits the State [of California] to authorize gambling on tribal land because the act [IGRA] contains no specific prohibition on such an action" (3).

Regardless of the outcome of the case, California's current gaming compact contains certain restrictions on tribal casinos.

THE SPECIFICS OF CALIFORNIA'S TRIBAL STATE COMPACT

Games Allowed

The following types of gambling are allowed in California Class III tribal casinos:

(1) Slot machines.
(2) Card games that are house banked (such as blackjack).
(3) Percentage card games (such as 5 card draw), where the house takes a percentage of the pot.
(4) Any game or device allowed under the California State Lottery.
(5) Off track betting. (California Tribal-State Gaming Compact)

Age Limitations

Casino players must be 18 years of age. If alcohol is served, then the minimum age is 21. (California Tribal-State Gaming Compact)

Compact Expiration

The California compact with tribes lasts 20 years. Renegotiation of allowable slot machines and revenue sharing (with tribes having no compact with the state) can occur after three years. (California Tribal-State Gaming Compact)

Restrictions

Each tribe with a compact is allowed a maximum of 2,000 slot machines. In addition, each tribe is limited to a maximum of two casinos. (California Tribal-State Gaming Compact)

Revenue Sharing Trust Fund

Tribes that operate more than 350 gaming devices will pay the following yearly amount into a trust fund for non-compacted tribes (California Tribal-State Gaming Compact):

Slot Machines	Fee/Device/Year
351-750	$900
751-1250	$1,950
1251-2000	$4,350

Also, a one-time fee of $1250 for each gaming device will be placed in the Revenue Sharing Trust Fund. Each non-compacted tribe will receive $1.1 million per year. If there is not enough money to distribute the full amount, then distribution will occur in equal amounts per tribe. For example, if there is only enough money for $900,000 per tribe, then that amount will be distributed. Anything in excess of $1.1 million will be dispersed in upcoming years. (California Tribal-State Gaming Compact)

Special Distribution Fund

The compact also calls for a Special Distribution Fund. The money distributed into this fund is based on the "average net win per device" (Ader, Falcone and Adam Steinberg 11). It will help cover:

- Administrative costs related to "programs designed to address gambling addiction".
- Help support state/local governments impacted by tribal gaming.
- Regulatory costs incurred by the state gaming agency.

The compact also notes that: "Contributions will be made in accordance with the following structure" (California Tribal-State Gaming Compact).

Slot Machines	Quarterly Contributions
1-200	0.0%
201-500	7.0% of net win
501-1000	10.0% of net win
1000-2000	13.0% of net win

Regulation

The tribe and the state will share equally in the regulatory control of Class III tribal casinos.

This section will end by stating that it is my intention to estimate the potential decrease in visitors to Reno/Sparks, based on proposed tribal casinos to be located around Sacramento, San Francisco and along the highways into the State of Nevada.

The next chapter titled, "(Reno/Sparks) Current Market" will analyze and evaluate the typical tourist to Reno/Sparks. It is not surprising that a majority of Reno's visitor base comes from Northern California.

In summary, this chapter indicates the following for the Northern Nevada/California Casino Economy:

✓ Northern Nevada casino operators should keep an eye on political developments occurring in California. A smooth harmonious relationship between California tribes and the State government could indicate that casinos will open faster than expected. On the other hand, bickering and arguments over sovereignty could stall the process of casino openings, therefore giving Nevada operators more time to prepare for additional competition.

- ✓ California tribes wishing to put a casino off reservation might have to make significant concessions to local governments and the state of California.

- ✓ If race/sports books begin operating in Oregon tribal casinos, then this could whittle away on Nevada's monopoly on this form of gaming entertainment.

- ✓ California tribes and state government might want to imitate Nevada's regulation and control methods. Nevada has already implemented most of the NGISC's recommendations regarding best practices for casino operations.

III. DEMOGRAPHICS FOR VISITORS TO RENO/SPARKS

The 1999 Reno-Sparks Visitor Profile Study is complied for the Reno-Sparks Convention and Visitors Authority by RRC Associates of Boulder, Colorado. More than 23,000 interviews were conducted over a ten-year period from 1990 to 1999. The report covers visitation patterns, tourist demographics, vacationer budgets and visitor views regarding the quality of the Reno/Sparks experience. The following graphs represent the highlights of that study.

HIGHLIGHTS

More than half of all visitors to Reno/Sparks are considered "empty nesters", meaning parents whose children no longer live at home (RSCVA 11).

FIGURE III-1: Percentage of Visitors to Reno/Sparks Considered "Empty Nesters" (12).

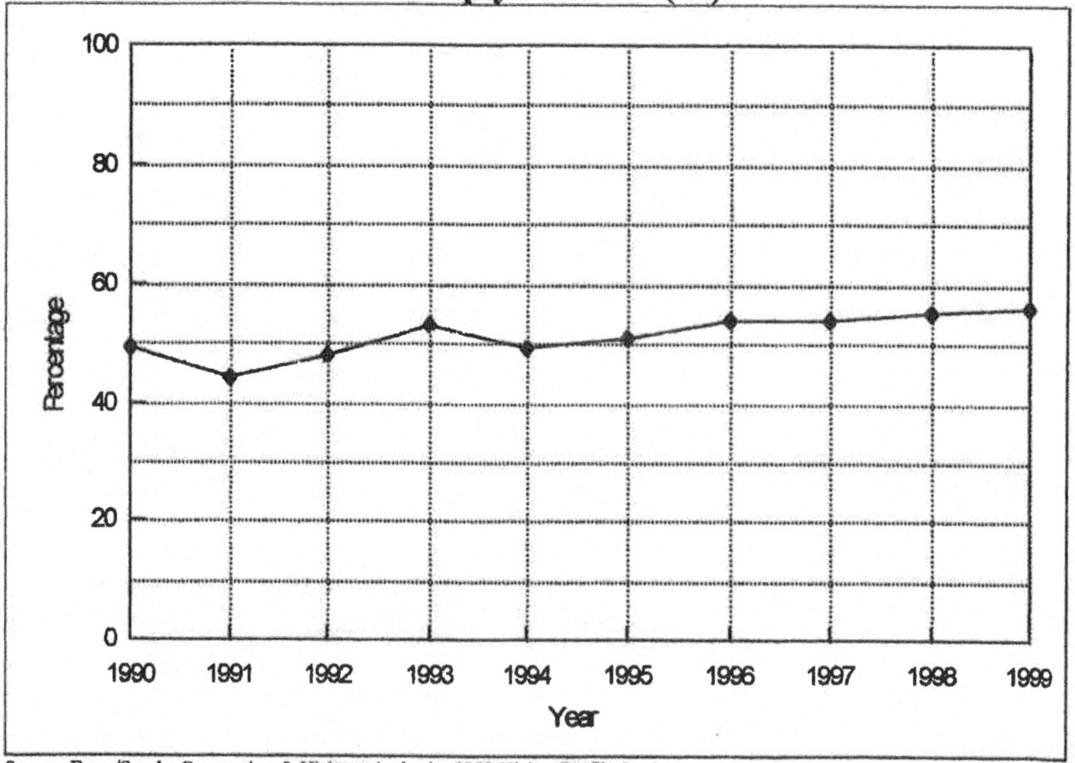

Source: Reno/Sparks Convention & Visitors Authority 1999 Visitor Profile Study

Likewise, the median age of the Average Reno/Sparks visitor tends to be over fifty years old, and it has been increasing over the past decade.

Figure III-2: Ten-Year Comparison, Median Age of the Reno/Sparks Visitor (12).

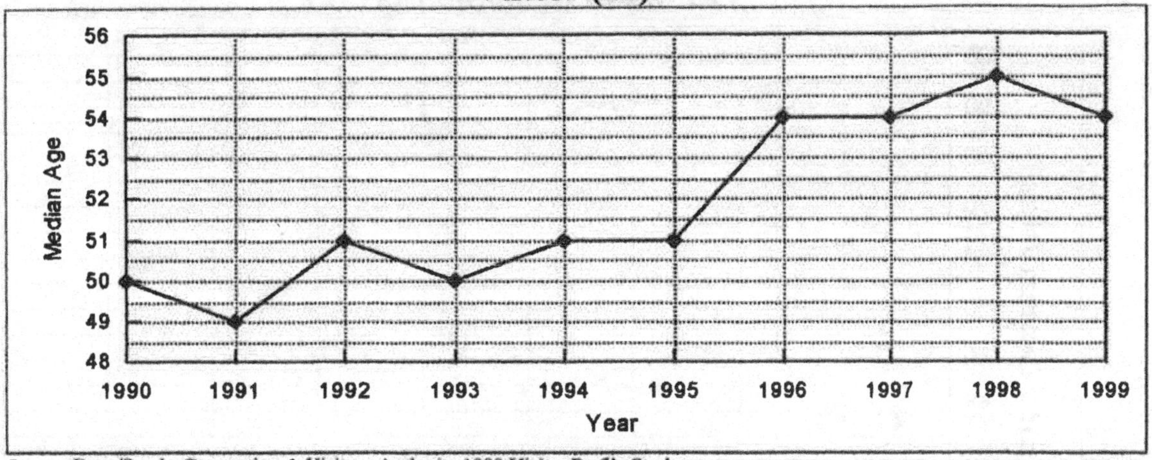

Source: Reno/Sparks Convention & Visitors Authority 1999 Visitor Profile Study

Year:	1990	1991	1992	1993	1994	1995	1996	1997	1998	1999
Median Age:	50	49	51	50	51	51	54	54	55	54

Figure III-3: Ten-Year Comparison, Percent of Reno/Sparks Visitors Over 50 Years of Age (12).

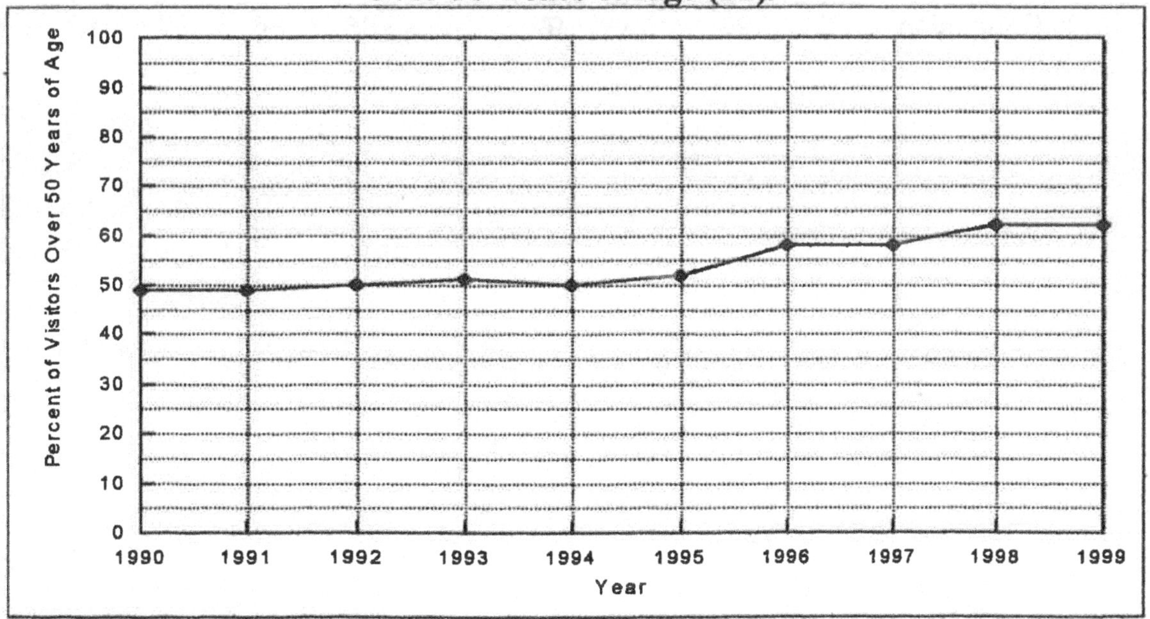

Source: Reno/Sparks Convention & Visitors Authority 1999 Visitor Profile Study

In addition, most of the visitors tend to be Caucasian and somewhat affluent.

FIGURE III-4: Ten-Year Comparison, Percentage of Caucasian Visitors to Reno/Sparks (12).

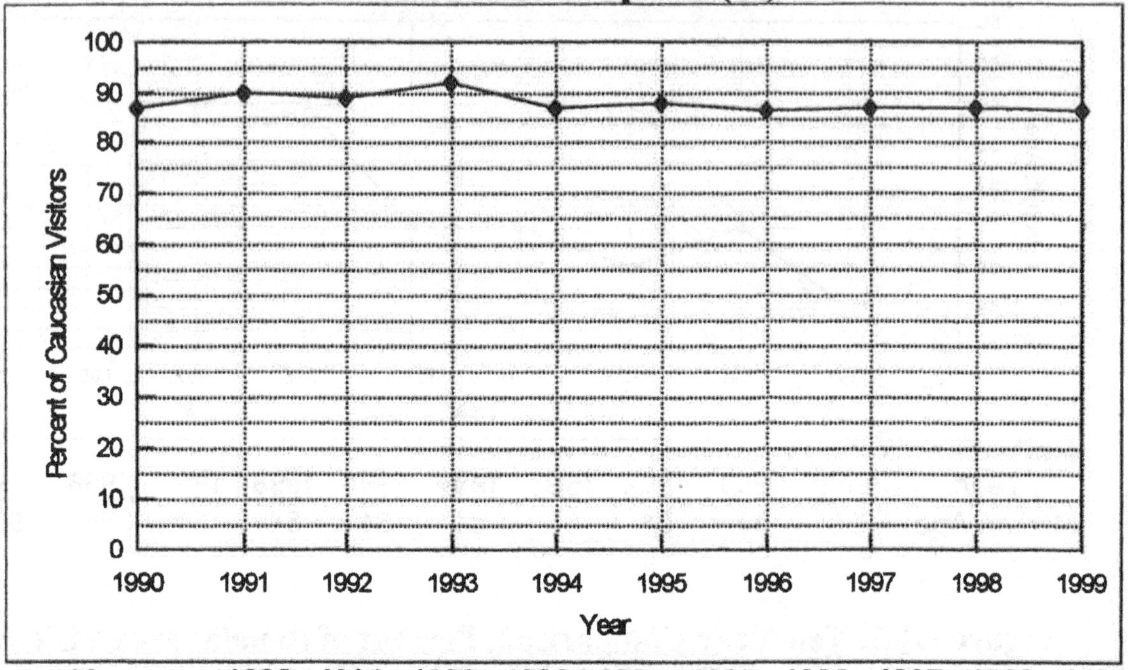

Year	1990	1991	1992	1993	1994	1995	1996	1997	1998	1999
% Caucasian	87	90	89	92	87	88	86	87	87	86

Figure III-5: Ten-Year Comparison, Median Household Income of the Reno/Sparks Visitor; Median Household Income of the United States Citizen. All Figures are in 1999 Dollars.

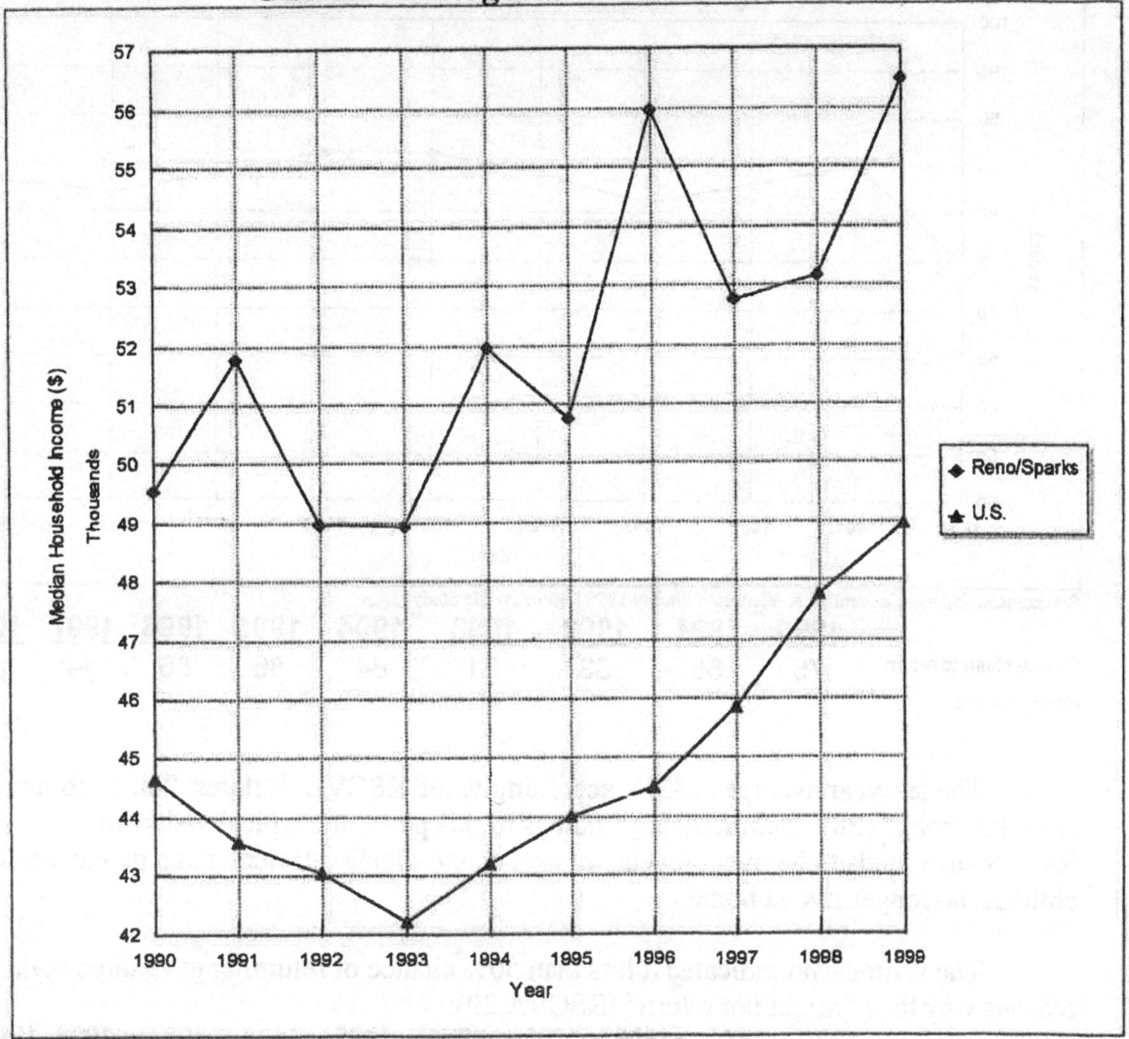

Sources: Reno/Sparks Convention & Visitors Authority 1999 Visitor Profile Study
Pingle

Year	1990	1991	1992	1993	1994	1995	1996	1997	1998	1999
Reno/Sparks	$49,553	$51,757	$48,975	$48,944	$51,963	$50,744	$55,963	$52,760	$53,162	$56,500
U.S.	$44,650	$43,556	$43,030	$42,219	$43,196	$43,986	$44,502	$45,836	$47,769	$48,950

Figure III-6: Ten-Year Comparison, Percentage of Tourists Who Claim They Will (definitely or very likely) Return to the Reno/Sparks Area within Two Years of Their Visit (12).

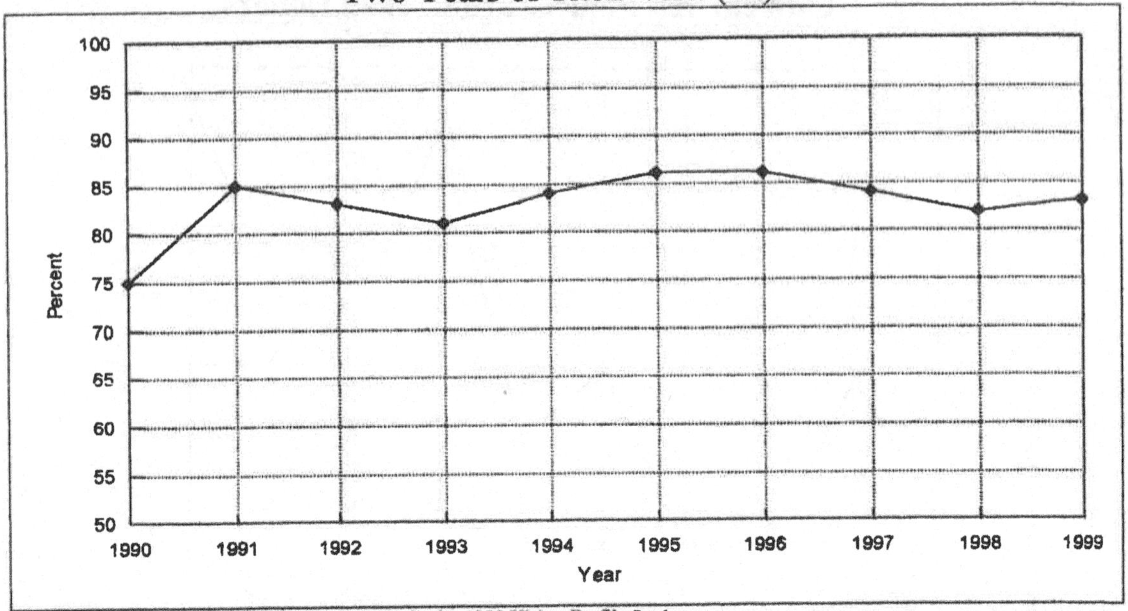

Source: Reno/Sparks Convention & Visitors Authority 1999 Visitor Profile Study

	1990	1991	1992	1993	1994	1995	1996	1997	1998	1999
% who claim to return within 2 years	75	85	83	81	84	86	86	84	82	83

The ten-year average is 83%; accordingly, the RSCVA declares, "intent to return remains strong" (28). Summarizing findings to this point, the typical visitor to Reno/Sparks tends to be over 50 years of age, economically affluent and a parent whose children no longer live at home.

The visitor who indicated a less than 50% chance of returning gave three main reasons why they "might not return" (RSCVA 29):

	1990	1991	1992	1993	1994	1995	1996	1997	1998	1999
(1) Too Far	16%	10%	13%	11%	17%	13%	19%	17%	16%	15%
(2) Other Plans	11%	11%	9%	5%	12%	11%	27%	23%	16%	26%
(3) Like to See Other Places	10%	9%	14%	18%	13%	14%	9%	11%	10%	9%

ANALYSIS OF KEY MARKETS

Half of all visitors to Reno/Sparks come from **California.**

Figure III-7: Ten Year Trend, Percentage of all Visitors to Reno/Sparks from California (4).

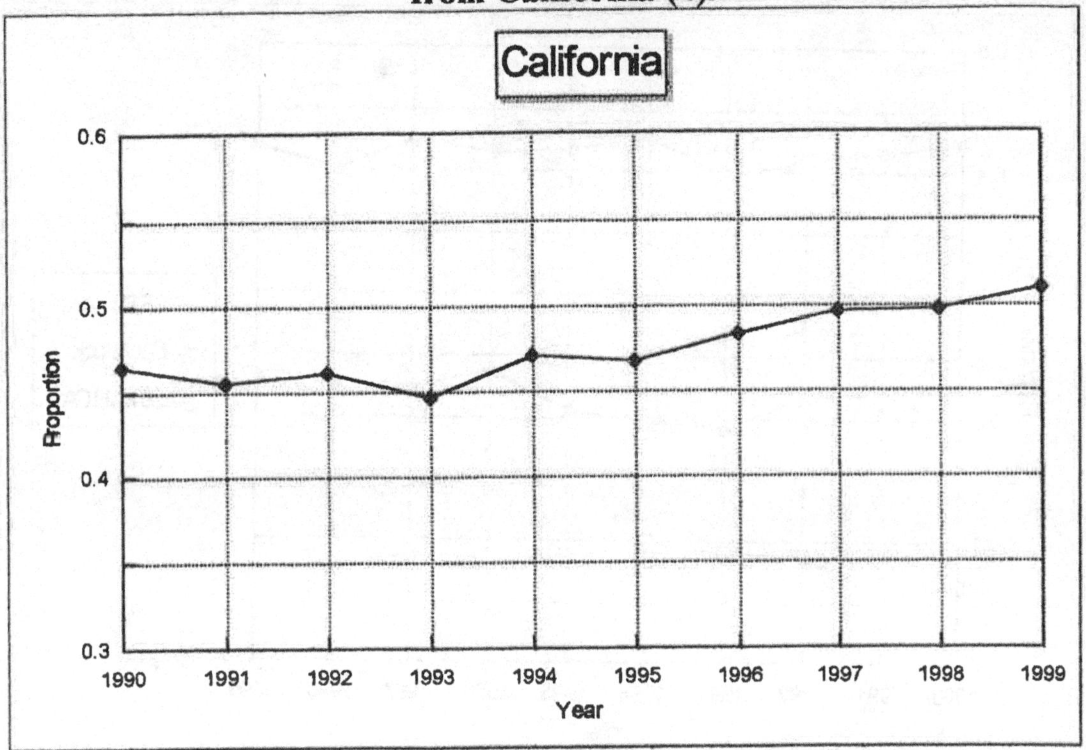

Source: Reno/Sparks Convention & Visitors Authority 1999 Visitor Profile Study

	1990	1991	1992	1993	1994	1995	1996	1997	1998	1999
California	46.4%	45.5%	46.1%	44.7%	47.1%	46.7%	48.3%	49.6%	49.8%	50.9%

Out of the visitors from California that arrive in Reno/Sparks, most come from the San Francisco Bay area, Sacramento/Stockton, or Northern California.

Figure III-8: Visitors to Reno/Sparks from California Markets (note: As a Percentage of Visitors from California only) (10).

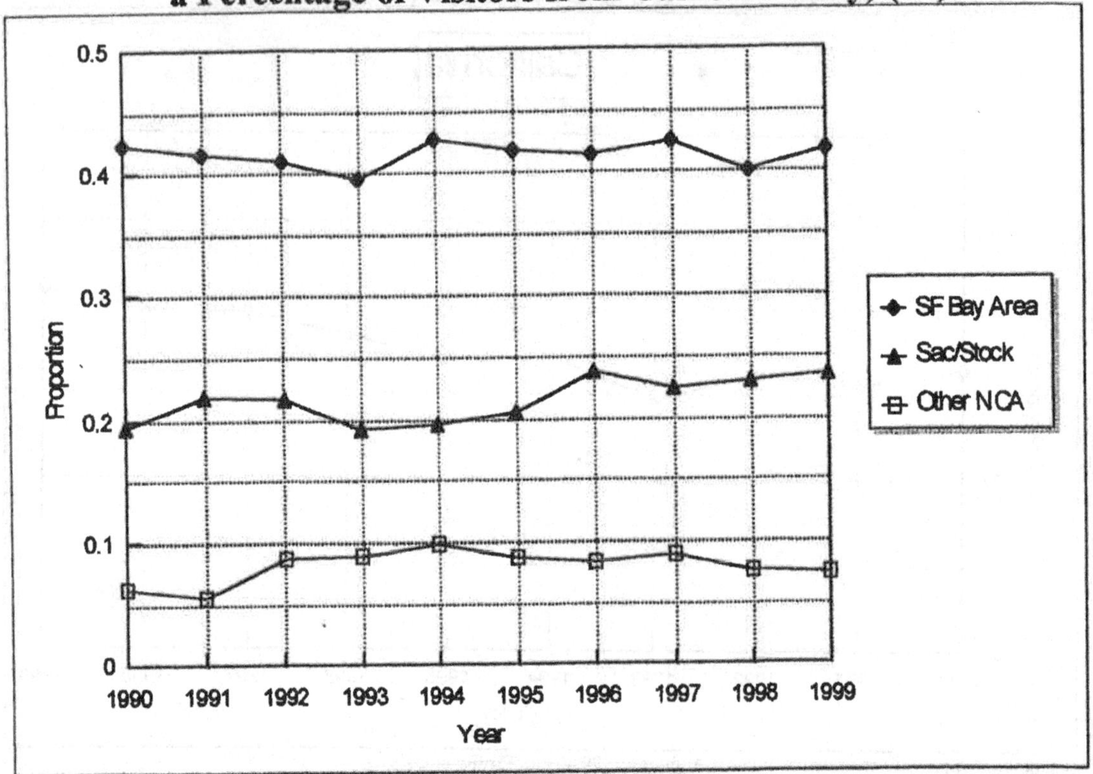

Source: Reno/Sparks Convention & Visitors Authority 1999 Visitor Profile Study

	1990	1991	1992	1993	1994	1995	1996	1997	1998	1999
SF Bay Area	42.3%	41.6%	41.0%	39.5%	42.6%	41.8%	41.3%	42.4%	40.0%	41.7%
Sac/Stock	19.3%	21.9%	21.7%	19.1%	19.6%	20.6%	23.7%	22.4%	23.0%	23.5%
Other N CA	6.2%	5.5%	8.6%	8.8%	9.8%	8.6%	8.3%	8.9%	7.5%	7.3%

As a matter of fact, history shows most visitors to Reno/Sparks arrive from Sacramento/Stockton and the Bay Area, either by private vehicle, RV or Bus.

Figure III-9: Ten-Year Comparison, Percentage of Visitors from the Sacramento/Stockton Area Who Arrive in Reno/Sparks via Private Vehicle, RV or Bus (45).

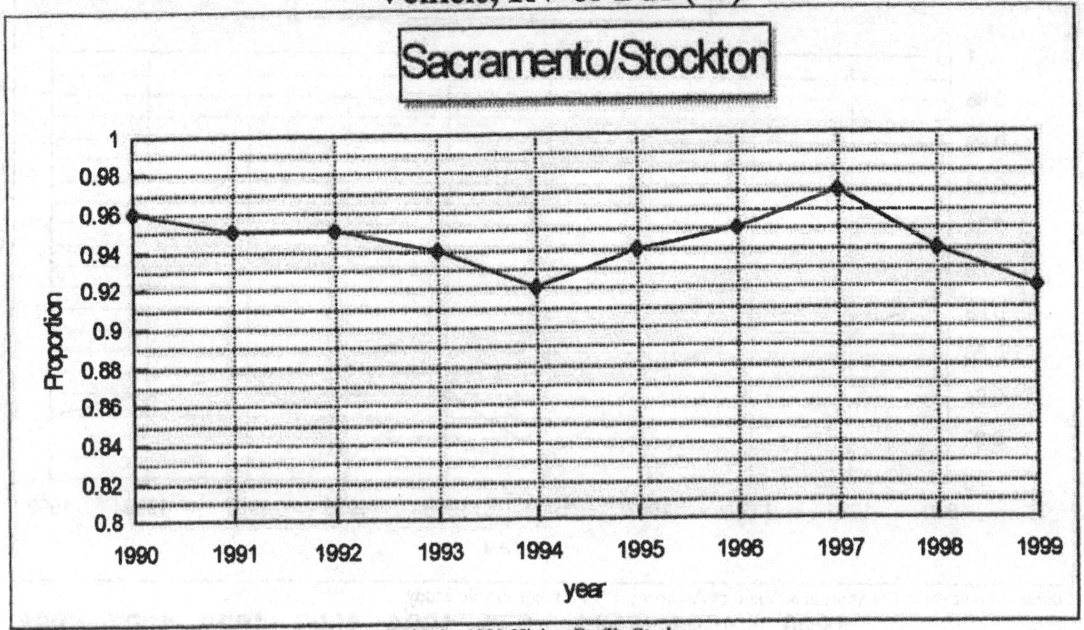

Source: Reno/Sparks Convention & Visitors Authority 1999 Visitor Profile Study

	1990	1991	1992	1993	1994	1995	1996	1997	1998	1999
Sac/Stock	96%	95%	95%	94%	92%	94%	95%	97%	94%	92%

Figure III-10: Ten-Year Comparison, Percentage of Visitors from the San Francisco Bay Area Who Arrive in Reno/Sparks via Private Vehicle, RV or Bus (45).

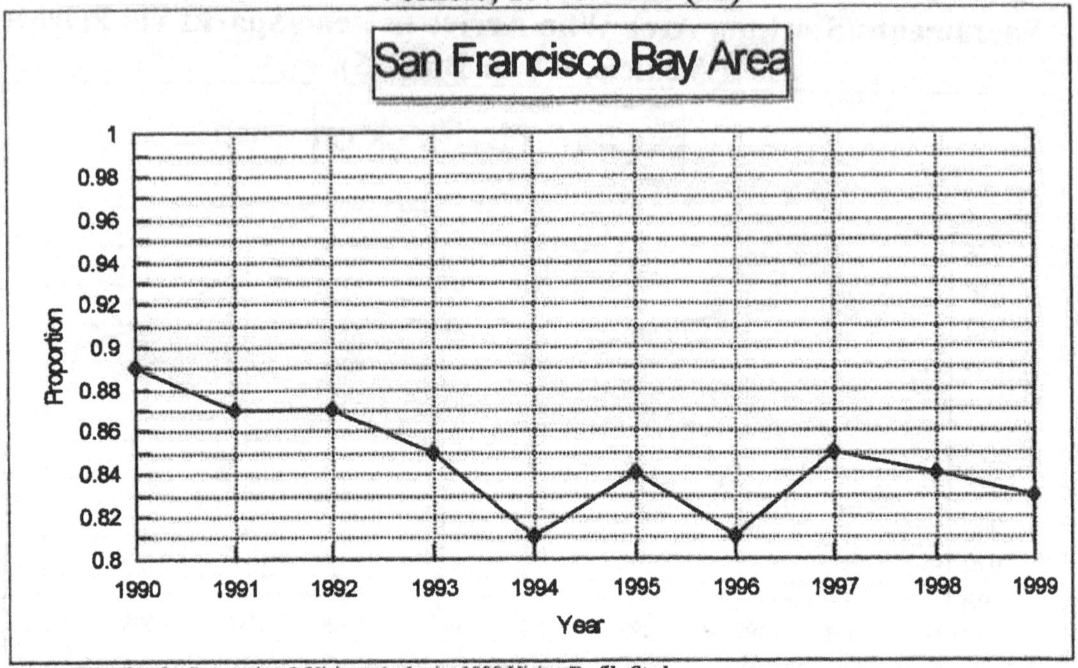

Source: Reno/Sparks Convention & Visitors Authority 1999 Visitor Profile Study

	1990	1991	1992	1993	1994	1995	1996	1997	1998	1999
SF Bay Area	89%	87%	87%	85%	81%	84%	81%	85%	84%	83%

The ten year trend indicates about 11% of the total visitors to Reno/Sparks arrive from the State of **Washington** (ES8).

Figure III-11: Percent of Total Visitors to Reno/Sparks From Washington State (ES-8).

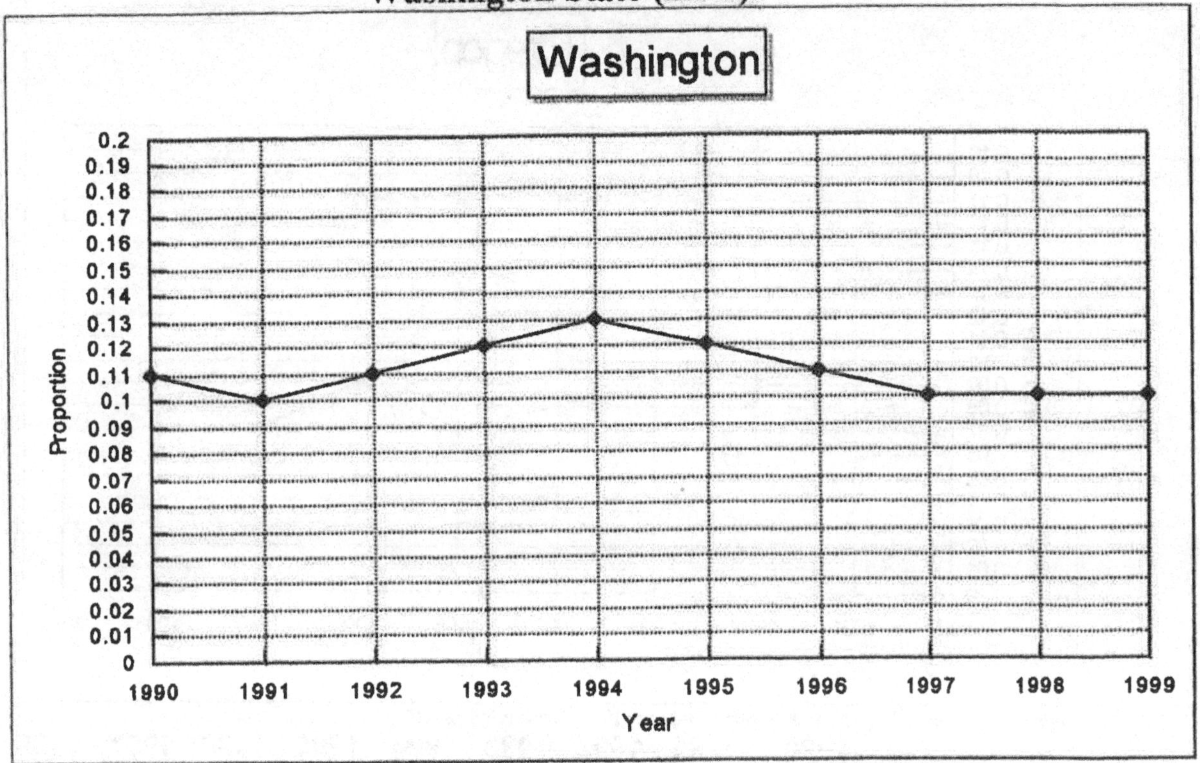

Source: Reno/Sparks Convention & Visitors Authority 1999 Visitor Profile Study

	1990	1991	1992	1993	1994	1995	1996	1997	1998	1999
Washington	11%	10%	11%	12%	13%	12%	11%	10%	10%	10%

About 8% of the Reno/Sparks market originates from **Oregon**.

Figure III-12: Percent of Total Visitors to Reno/Sparks from Oregon (ES 8).

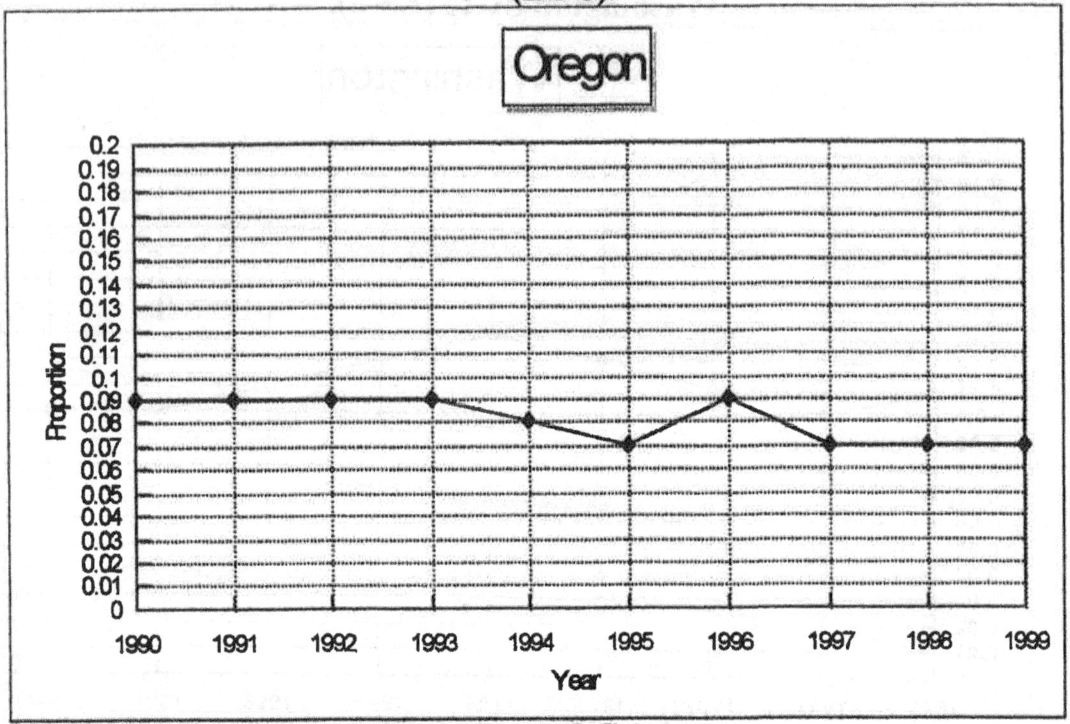

Source: Reno/Sparks Convention & Visitors Authority 1999 Visitor Profile Study

	1990	1991	1992	1993	1994	1995	1996	1997	1998	1999
Oregon	9%	9%	9%	9%	8%	7%	9%	7%	7%	7%

Visits from Canada have decreased in recent years. The RSCVA cites the following cause: an "unfavorable Canadian exchange rate" (ES 2).

Figure III-13: Percent of Total Visitors to Reno/Sparks from Canada (ES 8).

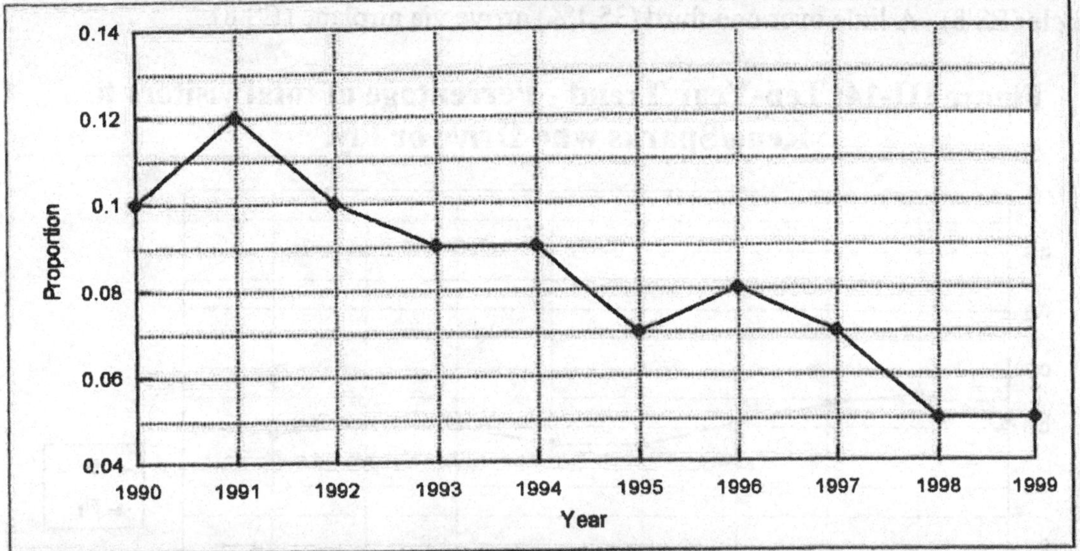

Source: Reno/Sparks Convention & Visitors Authority 1999 Visitor Profile Study

	1990	1991	1992	1993	1994	1995	1996	1997	1998	1999
Canada	10%	12%	10%	9%	9%	7%	8%	7%	5%	5%

It must also be kept in mind, slot machines and casino offerings in Canada, Washington, and Oregon might divert potential tourists from visiting Reno/Sparks.

PRIMARY METHOD OF TRAVEL TO RENO/SPARKS: over the past ten years, 60.6% of the visitors to Reno/Sparks have arrived via car, motorcycle, bus, or Recreational Vehicle (ES 8). A little over one-third (35.1%) arrive via airplane (ES 8).

Figure III-14: Ten-Year Trend - Percentage of total visitors to Reno/Sparks who Drive or Fly.

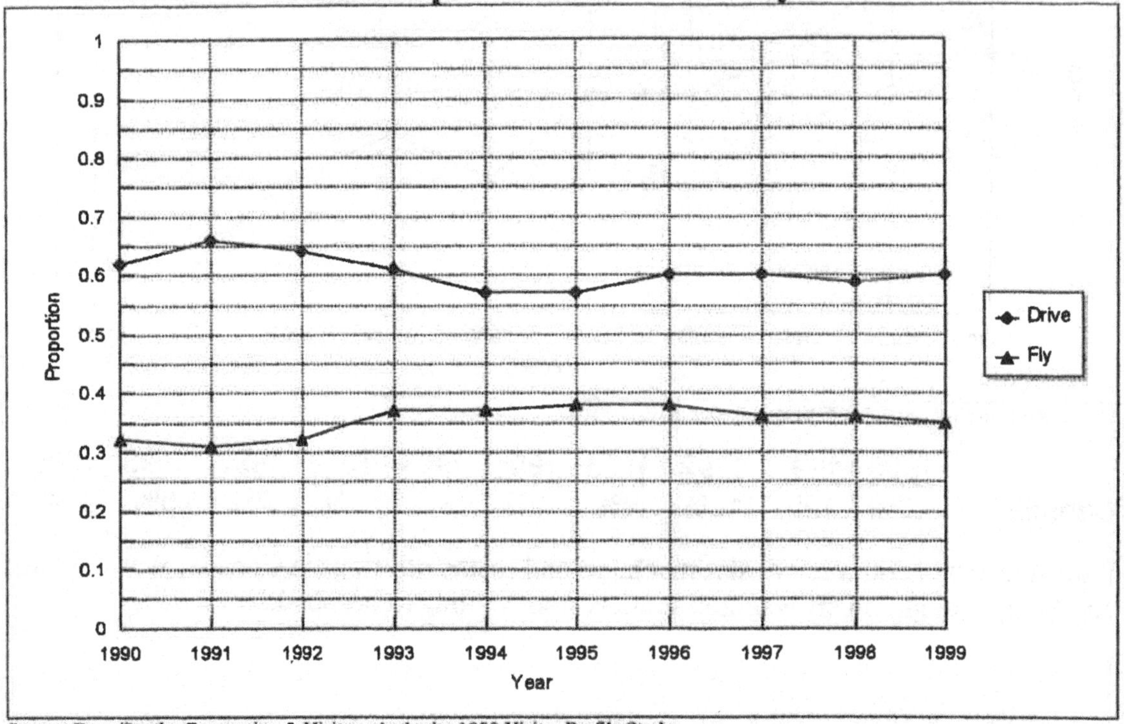

Source: Reno/Sparks Convention & Visitors Authority 1999 Visitor Profile Study

	1990	1991	1992	1993	1994	1995	1996	1997	1998	1999
Drive	62%	66%	64%	61%	57%	57%	60%	60%	59%	60%
Fly	32%	31%	32%	37%	37%	38%	38%	36%	36%	35%

ANALYSIS AND COMPARISON OF THE TOURIST WHO DRIVES TO RENO/SPARKS (Drive / Distance Ratio)[1]

Even though potential visitors who live closer to Reno/Sparks are more likely to visit Northern Nevada, a special attraction exists for the tourists from Redding, California; Monterey, California; Washington State and British Columbia, Canada.

In Summary, this chapter could indicate the following for the Northern Nevada/California Casino Economy:

- ✓ Reno/Sparks is becoming more dependent on the older, affluent, die-hard gambler; most of these tourists reside in California and arrive to Nevada via motor vehicle. These visitors might be more likely to substitute California tribal casinos for those in Reno/Sparks.
- ✓ Tribal casinos in Washington, Oregon and Western Canada have already sliced and could cut further into Reno/Sparks market share.
- ✓ Reno/Sparks receives more than double its fair share of tourists from Redding, California (217 miles away); about 1 ¾ of its fair share from Sacramento (134 miles away), Chico (165 miles away), and Stockton (179 miles away).[2] It appears Reno/Sparks displays a special attraction for the visitor from Redding. However, Redding now contains a tribal casino. It has been in operation since March 2000. This casino could divert the tourist from traveling to Reno/Sparks.
- ✓ Reno/Sparks receives its fair share (the drive/distance ratio is about 1.0) of visitors from Modesto, California (204 miles away) and the San Francisco Bay area (217 miles away).
- ✓ Reno/Sparks also appears to attract more driving visitors from far away Washington State and British Columbia, Canada than the closer California cities of San Diego, and Los Angeles. Again, some sort of attractions exists for these more distant travelers. On the other hand, increased casino offerings in these regions might reduce this loyalty to Northern Nevada.

---

[1]See Appendix B (following Chapter VI) for a complete discussion and analysis of Reno/Sparks typical driving visitor.

[2] Appendix B contains all the calculations.

CHAPTER IV: A MODEL TO ESTIMATE THE POTENTIAL IMPACT THAT NORTHERN CALIFORNIA TRIBAL GAMING WILL HAVE ON RENO/SPARKS.

The following assumptions are used to develop a model for Northern California tribal gaming and its potential impacts on the Reno/Sparks gaming economy:

(1) Past trends will be used in estimating future variables.

(2) Northern California casinos will serve as a substitute for casinos in Reno/Sparks.

(3) Reno/Sparks will face most of its competition from eight Northern California Casinos (Cache Creek, Casino San Pablo, Robertson Rancheria, Sho-Ka-Wah, Jackson Rancheria, Shingle Springs Rancheria, United Auburn Indian Community and Buena Vista Rancheria).

(4) All eight casinos will expand to their maximum allowable slot machines, 2000, and will be fully operational by January 1, 2004.

(5) The table games / slot ratio in Northern California will mimic that of Reno/Sparks.

(6) Only the driving (car, RV, motorcycle, bus) visitor from Sacramento, San Francisco, and Northern California who declares gaming as their primary trip purpose will be considered in the analysis.

(7) Any tourist coming from Los Angeles/Orange County or San Diego has put considerable thought into the trip. It is assumed that tribal casinos in California will not change their decision to visit Reno/Sparks. Besides, the number of visitors who drive from this market is not material.

Model

The preceding sections serve as a background to understanding Indian gaming in Northern Nevada's main feeder markets, along with Reno/Sparks' largest market of all, California.

A fairly stable long-term relationship exists between many of the model's variables, as noted above. These relationships will be held stable; future predictions will be made based on past data. Some relationships are unknown and must be estimated. For example, 79.3% of Sacramento/Stockton visitors declare gambling as the main purpose for visiting Reno/Sparks (Ader, Falcone, and Steinburg 54). The assumption will be made that most (but not all) of these potential tourists will be diverted to California Tribal casinos. This assumption could be made for a couple of reasons. First, California residents might substitute casino gaming in their own State for casino gaming in Nevada. Second, utility (satisfaction) could have an inverse relationship to the distance it takes to drive to a casino, i.e. everything being equal, one would rather drive one mile rather than 100 miles to reach a casino. Although this might sound like common sense, Thalheimer and Ali developed econometric models and found "the demand for wagering at a [gaming] facility was found to increase as access [. . .] increases" (2). Additional explanations in determination of the diversion estimate will be explained later in this essay. Of course, the reader is free to make another estimation and arrive at a different conclusion. The correct estimation of unknown variables should reveal what the future holds in store for the Reno/Sparks economy.

Among other sources, the Reno Sparks Convention and Visitors Authority (RSCVA) along with the Gaming Industry 1999/1998 statistical abstract provided a wealth of data (Leupp and Lee). It is my intention to convert this data into usable information. Nonetheless, past performance does not always guarantee future results. Also, rarely, does a model have the final word. The reader should be reminded that a model is only a simple explanation of a complex world. This simple explanation can be built upon, changed, and converted into a superior forecast. In other words, this section of the thesis must complement understanding, but not substitute for it.

Estimating Revenues of the Eight Northern California Casinos

Based on the assumptions of the model, Northern California will generate 43% more gaming revenue than Reno/Sparks with 37% fewer slot machines. A South African consulting firm, Corporate Image, published a paper on August 30, 1996 titled, "Structuring the Gaming Industry in the Public Interest". This paper focused on the South African tourist gaming industry and the potential impact on that country. The author of this paper declared, "Assumptions should focus on the [slot] machine side of the business" (Corporate Image 22). Furthermore, the same author argues attention should be paid to win/slot/day.

Win/slot/day estimates at California tribal casinos vary from $200 to $500 (Stearns E1). Five-year trend win/slot/day between 1995 and 2000 at the successful Connecticut tribal casinos (Foxwoods and Mohegan Sun) equals $372.49 (Leupp and Klein 78). A breakdown of win/slot/day for different locations is listed in table V-1.[1]

[1] Tables/Graphs V1 through V-10 can be found in Appendix D

A conservative estimate of win/unit/day for all California casinos is $200 (Stearns E3). In addition, generally accepted accounting principles suggest the most conservative approximation when figuring revenue. Accordingly, the average win/unit/day ($208.51) of all non-Nevada casinos will be used to estimate the potential revenues of Reno/Sparks 8 major competitors in Northern California. See the fourth column in table V-2.

Potential Loss in Visitors to Reno/Sparks from Northern California

Ten-year trends indicate 94.4% of Sacramento/Stockton visitors arrive in Reno via automobile, motorcycle, bus or RV. Over the past ten years, they represent 10.10% of Reno/Sparks total visitors. Along with that, most of these tourists (92.3%) stated they would "have a gaming expenditure" (RSCVA 90). Accordingly, if Reno/Sparks lost every visitor from Sacramento/Stockton, then 8.79% of its total gaming visitors would be sidetracked to tribal casinos in northern California.

This exercise was repeated for the San Francisco Bay Area, and the aggregate locations in Northern California. See table V-3.

Estimating the Number of Visitors to Reno/Sparks in 2004

A simple linear regression was performed based on the total visitors to Reno/Sparks from1990-1999. Based on the statistical trend, the total number of visitors in 2004 (without California tribal gaming) is projected at 5.5 million[2]. See graph V-4.

Based on the potential total percentage of visitors from Sacramento, San Francisco, and other areas in Northern California along with the total visitors to Reno/Sparks figured on a ten year trend, Reno/Sparks could expect, without gaming in California 840,090 tourists from San Francisco, 483,940 from Sacramento/Stockton and 416,862 from other areas in Northern California. See table V-5.

A point is reached in the model where another approximation must be made. Out of these potential driving visitors from Northern California, how many will be diverted to California Tribal Casinos? Once again, the RSCVA provides some guidance. For example, about 80.2% of SF Bay area residents declare gambling as their "primary trip purpose" (Ader 54). That same figure for Sacramento/Stockton is79.3% and (Northern) California on average is 77.9% (54). Even though Reno/Sparks will probably not lose 1,382,252 visitors from its Northern California market, one could conclude the higher the percentage of disposable income spent on gaming in California, the higher the likelihood of California tourist diversion. According to my calculations (see table V-6), the California citizen on average spends 0.77 percent of their disposable income (DI) on gaming entertainment. The average for the United States is 0.88 percent (table V-6). California tribal gaming will increase the number of gaming options and will likely increase the percentage of disposable income spent on gambling. Nevertheless, Oregon as a State has a large number of gambling options, as mentioned previously; it also ranks second to Nevada "in opportunities to gamble" (Gambling Magazine). Oregon residents spend 1.3% of their disposable income on gambling (table V-6). If California becomes

---

[2] It should be noted that a log linear regression resulted in a lower coefficient of multiple determination, and lower t value, therefore it was not used.

like Oregon in regard to opportunities to gamble, then one could expect California to spend 0.91 percent of their disposable income on casino gambling (table V-6):

1.2861%-.3773%=.9088 or .91%

Forecasted % of DI spent on gaming-% spent on non casino gaming=%DI spent on casino gaming

Substitution of California Casinos for Nevada Casinos

A forecasted percentage of disposable income spent on gambling will assist in the calculation of a diversion rate for Northern California visitors traveling to Reno/Sparks. If trends hold constant, Californians in 1999 lost approximately $3.25 billion in Nevada casinos:

$25,100 x 33,145,121 x .3912 % = $3,254,559,205

Per Capita DI x CA population x % of DI spent on gambling = amount spent in NV casinos

Again, it must be understood: Californians being diverted from Nevada casinos to California tribal casinos is an unknown figure. It is unlikely that diversion would be 100%; accordingly, it is not probable there would be no diversion. An additional assumption will be made: Northern California driver diversion from Reno/Sparks casinos will equal the substitution percentage if Nevada as a State retains its original revenues from California. This might represent the worst-case scenario for the Reno area. Under this assumption, the expected diversion would equal 56.95%. See table V-7.

If this assumption is reliable, then the Reno/Sparks market would lose over 787,000 visitors annually by 2004-2005. Again, see table V-5.

In addition, if trends in the past hold true into the future, then the average San Francisco Bay area tourist stays 1.9 days; the same figure for Sacramento/Stockton is 1.6 and other Northern California visitors stay 1.8 days. The data in this paragraph are noted/summarized in table V-5.

Again, if past trends stay consistent in regard to gaming, food and beverage, lodging, retail, shows, sightseeing, recreation and special events, then the per day expenditures can be expected from visitors in San Francisco, Sacramento/Stockton, and Northern California as noted at the end of table V-5. This is extended into per trip amounts as listed in table V-5b.

If the expected loss in visitors is multiplied by the trended amounts spent per person per trip, then the figures at the end of table V-5b come to light. Also, 56.95% for whatever reason might not be the correct diversion rate. Expected loss in revenues for various digression rates can be found in table V-8.

An Analysis of an Increase in the Number of Gaming Options

The issue confronting the Reno/Sparks market parallels the competitive impact when a new casino opens in a mature market. Two such examples can be examined in Reno and in Atlantic City.

The Silver Legacy Resort Casino opened in Reno during July of 1995 and added over 2000 slot machines to the market (Table/Graph V-9). It appears the increase in supply resulted in a decrease of $2.58 in win/slot/day. However, win/slot/day began to catch up and then surpass its 1994-1995 level by 1998 (Table/Graph V-9). This shows resilience to an increase in the number of gaming options. Atlantic City, on the other hand paints a different picture. See Table/Graph V-10.

From the opening of the Trump Taj Mahal in 1990, and then the subsequent expansion of permitted slot machines in other Atlantic City casinos generally resulted in a decrease in win/slot/day. This shows non-resilience to an increase in the number of gaming options. Also, remember all figures have been adjusted for inflation; all amounts are in 1999 dollars.

V. CONCLUSION

If the salient points of this thesis were distilled up to this point, then the following deductions could be made:

- ✓ Politics, not economics, plays a greater role in Class II and Class III tribal gaming.
- ✓ According to the assumptions of the model, Reno/Sparks will lose over $279 million in gaming revenue and over $124 million in other proceeds between 2004-2005. Bear Stearns estimates that Reno/Sparks will lose $231.6 million or 22% of expected gaming revenues between 2004-2005 (Ader, Falcone and Steinberg 57). In addition, Curtis and Rose predict a 17.7% reduction in Northwest Nevada gaming revenue (16).

These last two chapters indicates the following for the Northern Nevada/California Casino Economy:

- ✓ California tribal gaming could have a huge impact on the Reno/Sparks economy. Also, Northern California might expect a migration of workers previously employed by Nevada casinos. Although it might be easy to acquire the skills of the average casino worker, the typical Nevada hospitality employee has years of experience in his/her chosen field. This might give the Nevadan an edge in employment.

- ✓ Casino gaming has spread once again; it also appears that several tribes in Northern California will enjoy economic benefits. According to the assumptions of this model, Reno/Sparks will lose $279 million in gaming revenue, but Northern California is expected to gain gaming revenues of $3.2 billion.

- ✓ Reno/Sparks as a whole should prepare marketing strategies to deal with defending its current market share and securing additional guests. First and foremost, Nevada operators must recognize the intangible production nature of gaming. Second, strategies must be developed to provide the guest with what he really desires via market research, employee training, and management's recognition of culture as an important tool. Third, memorable experiences must be created for the casino guest. These three points will be touched upon in the next chapter.

- ✓ A conclusion could not be made in regard to Reno/Sparks gaming resilience. This was displayed in two different mature market examples.

RENO'S SWOT

Before moving on to recommendations, an inventory will be taken of Reno's strengths, weaknesses, opportunities, and threats.

- STRENGTHS:
  Reno has a close proximity to non-gaming attractions such as skiing, golf, Virginia City, Lake Tahoe, hiking and mountain biking.

  There are a wide variety of casinos located fairly adjacent to each other.

- WEAKNESSES
  Reno is a mature gaming market facing significant competition, namely from Las Vegas, Northern California, Oregon, and Washington.

  Downtown Reno has a seedy reputation.

  Methods of management are passed down from generation to generation and might have become stagnant.

  There is a general non-recognition of the service nature of gaming entertainment.

- OPPORTUNITIES
  Reno/Sparks can create and promote a "positive brand awareness" for the area (RSCVA).

  The Reno area can market towards the younger population segment (age 25-54).

  Reno can clean up the seedy image of its downtown area.

- THREATS
  Tribal gaming in Northern California, Washington and Oregon could divert tourists who would usually travel to Reno/Sparks.

  Hard-core casino gamblers, especially those in Northern California, now have more options.

The following suggestions will address some of these issues.

VI: RECOMMENDATIONS

Tribal casino gaming in California may succeed and flourish and its full potential might be realized. On the other hand, perhaps the card clubs will have their way, and Indian casinos will be shut down, never to open again in California. The second scenario, however, is politically unlikely. This chapter's aim is to assist Reno/Sparks casino operators in accomplishing the following:

- Defending its current market shares and/or
- Securing additional guests

General Nature/Characteristics of Services

First and foremost, gambling, from a production/marketing standpoint is entertainment. Entertainment is a service. Gaming is often coupled with hospitality, another service. Different rules of production/marketing apply to services.

Along with that, due to the general nature of services it should be noted that the numbers on figure III-6 (tourists who claim they will definitely or very likely return to Reno/Sparks) could be over- inflated. Zeithaml makes a number of key observations in her book, *Marketing of Services* (Bowen). First of all, casinos sell hospitality and entertainment. These goods are for the most part intangible, as all services are. Coins will be deposited into a slot machine or bets placed on a craps table with the hope of a financial return. However, there is an all important service aspect that goes along with these wagers. Along with the bet, the patron purchases the friendliness of the dealer and the change person's willingness to display a sincere smile. This is an aspect of value that goes along with visiting a casino.

Keep in mind, no warranty exists in making a wager. The patron might win or lose. Also, nothing says that the service employee will be friendly. On the other hand, "[Tangible] goods carry warranties or guarantees with purchase, emphasizing that the producer believes that if something goes wrong, it is not the fault of the consumer" (Bowen 23).

When a consumer purchases a toaster, computer, or automobile, the item is already produced. Services, on the other hand, are often produced and consumed at the same time. The consumer must provide a clear definition of what is desired. A guest must tell a waiter how he wants his steak cooked. A casino patron might not effectively communicate her wishes to the service staff. It very well could be the gambler's fault for not obtaining the satisfaction she desires; she did not provide a clear definition in the first place. Zeithaml proposes:

- ✓ Consumers attribute some of their dissatisfaction with services to their own inability to specify or perform their part of the service (23).

- ✓ Consumers may complain less frequently about services than about products due to their belief that they themselves are partly responsible for their dissatisfaction (23).

Due to these reasons, satisfaction with services might be lower than surveys reveal. The same holds true with the Reno/Sparks experience.

Also, services differ from tangible physical items (cars, stereos, shoes, computers, etc.) in the following ways. First, as mentioned previously, services are for the most part intangible. This product cannot be "physically possessed" (Skinner 351). In addition, service qualities cannot be evaluated through the five senses. Although it is hard to evaluate services, judgments can be made based on physical (tangible) surroundings. For example, walking into the Mirage Hotel/Casino in Las Vegas and viewing the surroundings (aquarium behind the front desk, marble floors, atrium, etc.) might provide some clues to the level of service expected. It should be noted that not all wares are purely tangible or purely intangible. Table VI-1 (located on page 97) makes some distinctions. A visit to the local, or far away, casino probably falls in the middle of Chart VI-1. Entertainment is not a pure service, but not a purely tangible item either. However, the table does rank entertainment high in experience qualities.

This leads into the next point. Services, especially those difficult to evaluate and high in experience qualities, often cannot be separated from consumption and production. In other words, a service is created and used at the same time. The casino patron helps produce the service, perhaps by placing a wager; he then receives entertainment out of the transaction. Therefore enjoyment is created and produced simultaneously

Due to the inseparable nature of a service, both the provider and consumer play an important role in its delivery. The consumer must be clear and concise as to what he desires out of the transaction.

Providing an example in the casino industry, a blackjack player must be sure to communicate to the dealer what he desires (hit, stay, split, double down). The dealer must also know the rules of the game and be able to efficiently deal the game.

Because services are produced and consumed at the same time, they are quite perishable. Unused capacity cannot be stored for future use. An empty roulette seat, an unoccupied hotel room, or unused slot machine on Thanksgiving cannot be stored for use on New Year's Eve. The perishability aspect always deals with time sensitivity. Managers on all levels should take this characteristic of service into account.

Services are also, for the most part, labor intensive. Because people, and not machines, perform services, inconstancy and variation have a tendency to run rampant. As an example, two employees with the same education, same training, and same experience, working at the same time, can give two different levels of service performance. Lack of standardization might, on the surface, appear to be a problem, but just the opposite could be the case. Heterogeneity allows the shrewd and insightful casino to perform market research, recognize the needs of the guest, and shape services to satisfy those desires. Even so, Albrecht and Zemke in their book titled "Service America" continually restate the following observation: what the consumer/guest wants could be quite different from what a service provider *thinks* the guest wants.

When it comes to market research, each casino property must first take its individual corporate culture into account. This paper will not be able to take the place of a study on the subject of market research. Nonetheless, any Reno/Sparks casino operator should know, beyond a shadow of a doubt, what his/her patron desires through "a program for managing and organizing information gathered from inside and outside [their] organization" (Skinner 279).

After defining the concern, whatever it may be, a strategy must be designed for performing study and exploration. The researcher should obtain data on the subject or gather facts via survey, interview, or observation. The findings should then be analyzed, interpreted, and reported. Again, the reader is strongly urged to look into the area of market research. Finding out what the guest really wants is an essential element of providing it.

Market research, alone, will not improve service. Discovering what the consumer really wants is an essential first step, but probably will not "create a customer orientated organization, a customer friendly system [or] a work environment that reinforces the idea of putting the customer first" (Albrecht & Ron Zemke 27). Albrecht and Zemke also stress the importance of "moment of truth" management/identification (27). A "moment of truth" is defined as: "An episode in which a customer comes into contact with any aspect of [a] company, however remote, and thereby has an opportunity to form an impression" (27).

Summarizing the nature of services thus far: "moments of truth" have to be identified and managed, market research should also be performed to help ensure the guest's needs are being met, and the casino should realize the difference between the production of tangible vs. intangible goods.

Pine and Gilmore in their book titled "The Experience Economy" see a definite relationship between commodities, tangible goods and intangible services, but take the idea of production one step further. They venture into the arena of what they define as a "memorable experience" (Pine and Gilmore 11). This has four parts.

To begin with, Pine and Gilmore see commodities as items that are mined, excavated or grown. They also consider commodities "fungible" meaning "they are what they are" (6). Examples of commodities could include wood, metal, silicone and paper. Because no/very little differentiation exists with a commodity, they react easily to supply and demand.

Secondly, Pine and Gilmore observe that commodities are used "as raw materials" to produce goods (7). They define goods as "tangible items sold to largely anonymous customers who [usually] buy them off the shelf, from the lot [or] out of the catalog [. . .]" (7). Goods can be put to use immediately, hence valued more than the commodities where they came from. Examples of goods include a deck of cards, a pair of dice, a slot machine or a roulette table.

Third, Pine and Gilmore see that goods become services, therefore intangible "when customized to the individual request of known clients" (8). Examples include a dealer using a deck of cards, roulette wheel, or pair of dice to satisfy the entertainment desires of casino patrons. Instead of sitting home and obtaining entertainment by playing chess, checkers, solitaire or *trivial pursuit*, the casino patron is willing to pay a premium to obtain amusement via the house advantage. It must be remembered: the difference between good and service can become quite blurry. For example, a restaurant serves food and drink; both of these are tangible items. However, economists place restaurant meals in the service category because different restaurants portray various themes. In addition, each meal is "delivered on demand in response to an individual patron's order" (8). Likewise, even though casino games are basically the same, the theme of a gaming establishment could be considered different from its competitor. Also, wagering requests (via blackjack, craps, race/sports books, slot machine, roulette wheel, etc) are "delivered on demand in response to an individual patron's order" (8).

Forth, Pine and Gilmore consider the perfect blending of "service as [a] stage and goods as props" in the production of a "memorable experience" (11-12). The person who purchases an experience is not a customer but a "guest" (12). This experience is "rich with sensation" (12). Also, "no two people can have the same experience" (12).

Training could be used as a tool to handling moment of truth protocol and producing memorable experiences, but getting people to change status quo methods of management is no easy chore. Management beliefs of employees on every level are, for the most part, set in stone. When suggesting change, one will surely hear the phrase, "But, that's the way its always been done."

Actually, there is a lot behind this commonly heard expression. The area of institutional economics helps explain why an old, outdated, method is usually preferred to a new, superior, process. When one hears the word "institution," one of two things usually comes to mind:

- ✓ Mental hospital or
- ✓ A for-profit financial organization

Although these might be two meanings of "institutions," the economist holds a different definition: "Institutions are the rules of the game in a society or, more formally, are the humanly devised constraints that shape human interaction" (North 3).

Rules (aka institutions) make things more certain, but more importantly give "structure to everyday life" (3). Just to give an example: it would be difficult to play a craps game if the rules changed after every roll of the dice. Another example: an entrepreneur in Hawaii could make a lot of money by offering an underground casino. However, state and federal laws are established that make such a proposition illegal. Laws are what institutional economists consider formal institutions. The rules of craps, and the non-acceptance of casino gaming in Hawaii, guide and limit acceptable (economic) choices. Both of the above circumstances are examples of formal institutions.

Other examples of formal institutions include the Nevada Revised Statutes, the Michigan State Constitution, and the policies listed in a casino employee handbook. In addition, institutions might evolve, like common law.

One might expect formal rules to be the most important source of limitations that form acceptable options. Nothing could be further from the truth. Culture (an integrated pattern of human knowledge, belief, and behavior that depends on man's capacity for learning and transmitting knowledge to succeeding generations) provides an even stronger evolutionary institution: informal rules (M-W.com and North). Culture and informal rules help humans in explaining and understanding the world around us. In addition, culture (man's tendency to transmit knowledge via imitation) "provides continuity so that the informal solution to [. . .] problems in the past carries over into the present" (North 37).

These informal rules (that stem from culture) shape into a belief system. This belief system, once created, has extraordinary staying power. Beliefs are never "consciously designed" but they are usually "in everyone's interest to keep" (41). Examples include standard weights/measures, rules of the road and the QWERTY typewriter layout (41). An informal rule/belief in the casino industry might be the idea of "paying ones dues" before achieving career advancement.

The power of beliefs should never be under estimated. As an example, religion and ideas on economic systems (capitalism vs. communism) give countless examples. Beliefs can also lead to extreme sacrifices (again note the subject of religion); this occurs because commonly held ideas provide structure. However, even an incorrect belief provides that same structure. Anyone not accepting a commonly held, although erroneous, belief could face severe sanctions.

To sum up, why does the phrase "because that's the way it's always been done" hold so much power that other methods of production might not even be considered?

(1) Firms set out on a path dependent on a belief system. This belief system provides structure to everyday interactions. Extreme sacrifices will be made for beliefs, even if they turn out to be incorrect. Beliefs stem from informal rules. However, more importantly, informal rules originate from culture. Culture could be summarized as learned, imitated behavior, passed down from generation to generation. Generation to generation might be adult-to-offspring, veteran police officer-to-rookie or seasoned casino executive-to-newly promoted supervisor. Learned, imitated behavior is simply the way it's always been done.
(2) Institutions, in general, simplify life and provide a guide to everyday human interaction and daily economic exchange.
(3) Repeated situations give way to a standard method of handling those situations.

The way something has always been done is merely the prevailing approach. A casino wishing to bring about change can take advantage of the nature of institutions and promote operational modifications by doing so in tiny incremental steps. These infinitesimal adjustments will not likely engage employee defense mechanisms. Trying to make sweeping changes overnight could be perceived as an attempt to attack belief systems.

On-going, continuous training is very important because it can help change belief systems in a slow and deliberate manner. In addition, it would be virtually impossible to keep an eye on every direct labor employee 24 hours a day, 7 days a week, 365 days a year. If the front line employee knows the correct procedure, is given empowerment authority, is provided with on-going training and also maximizes every moment of truth to produce memorable experiences, then the Reno/Sparks economy might earn a reputation as being the most service-orientated gaming destination. This reputation, once earned and reinforced, would be hard to shake.

I intend to propose the following: California casinos could have a significant impact on the Reno/Sparks gaming economy. Casino executives, managers, and supervisors have traditionally assumed that they know what the guest wants when it comes to service. It should be noted that Sherlock Holmes makes a good point when he says, "There is nothing so deceptive as an obvious fact" (Albrecht and Zemke 60). If a casino wants to know what the guest really desires, then market research should be performed.

Performing research and knowing what the casino patron wants will not help if there is no method for delivering it to them. Posting signs urging employees to give good service probably won't do any good (again, a method must be provided). On the other hand, training employees to recognize moments of truth, respond accordingly to guest desires, and produce memorable experiences could make or break the long-term profitability of a casino.

According to Connellan and Zemke, it costs 4 to 7 times as much to create a customer as it does to maintain a customer (Bowen 1). A dissatisfied customer/guest, for whatever reason, will tell an average 20 people about their experience. However, a satisfied customer/guest will, on average, only tell 8 others about their positive encounter (Bowen). That means it takes 2 ½ satisfied customers to make up for one who is not content.

In summary and conclusion, my final recommendation is for Reno/Sparks casinos to organize their efforts and form a loose confederation to achieve a common objective: promote Reno/Sparks as the destination for superior memorable service. In conjunction with this, each casino should intensify efforts to satisfy guest needs via market research, manage moments of truth, train employees and produce memorable experiences. It must be remembered that these efforts could be stymied if corporate culture prevents change from occurring.

APPENDIX A: FIVE-YEAR TREND, WIN/UNIT/DAY

	year	number of slots	win/unit/ day	win/unit/ day in 1999 dollars	win/unit/ day for all slots (1999 $)	slot hold
Atlantic City	1999	35,679	$226.98	$226.98	$8,098,419	8.20%
	1998	35,474	$218.19	$221.79	$7,867,697	8.40%
	1997	33,806	$220.45	$226.72	$7,664,626	8.40%
	1996	31,250	$229.59	$240.61	$7,519,073	8.40%
	1995	28,496	$247.35	$264.24	$7,529,881	8.50%
	Atlantic City Averages:			$234.84		8.37%
Colorado	1999	13,633	$105.55	$105.55	$1,438,963	5.50%
	1998	13,086	$95.11	$96.68	$1,265,132	5.70%
	1997	13,092	$84.84	$87.25	$1,142,336	5.90%
	1996	12,536	$83.82	$87.84	$1,101,204	6.00%
	1995	12,398	$78.39	$83.74	$1,038,256	6.30%
	Colorado Averages:			$92.45		5.87%
Connecticut	1999	8,839	$379.75	$379.75	$3,356,610	n/a
	1998	8,624	$354.14	$359.98	$3,104,462	n/a
	1997	7,908	$327.38	$336.70	$2,662,600	n/a
	1996	4,899	$372.30	$390.17	$1,911,445	n/a
	1995	3,870	$406.79	$434.57	$1,681,797	n/a
	Connecticut Averages:			$372.49		n/a
Delaware	1999	3,584	$310.26	$310.26	$1,111,972	7.60%
	1998	2,709	$355.76	$361.63	$979,645	7.70%
	1997	2,567	$319.85	$328.95	$844,422	7.60%
	1996	1,700	$295.52	$309.70	$526,498	7.90%
	Delaware Averages:			$327.89		7.67%
Illinois	1999	8,277	$352.43	$352.43	$2,917,063	n/a
	1998	8,060	$284.67	$289.36	$2,332,273	n/a
	1997	8,078	$264.26	$271.78	$2,195,444	n/a
	1996	8,011	$276.07	$289.32	$2,317,753	n/a
	1995	7,746	$286.48	$306.05	$2,370,632	n/a
	Illinois Averages:			$302.03		n/a

(cont. on next page)

source: Gaming Industry 1999 Statistical Abstract

	year	number of slots	win/unit/ day	win/unit/ day in 1999 dollars	win/unit/ day for all slots (1999 $)	slot hold
Indiana	1999	14,817	$223.67	$223.67	$3,314,118	n/a
	1998	12,456	$226.09	$229.82	$2,862,613	n/a
	1997	9,099	$210.80	$216.80	$1,972,656	n/a
	1996	3,608	$201.31	$210.97	$761,190	n/a
	1995	90	$130.77	$139.70	$12,573	n/a
	Indiana Averages:			$222.69		n/a
Iowa	1999	7,140	$167.89	$167.89	$1,198,735	n/a
	1998	6,822	$160.50	$163.15	$1,112,985	n/a
	1997	6,203	$152.85	$157.20	$975,112	n/a
	1996	6,003	$135.77	$142.29	$854,149	n/a
	1995	3,540	$139.85	$149.40	$528,881	n/a
	Iowa Averages:			$157.19		n/a
Missouri	1999	14,975	$137.55	$137.55	$2,059,811	n/a
	1998	14,730	$123.10	$125.13	$1,843,162	n/a
	1997	14,031	$107.06	$110.11	$1,544,909	n/a
	1996	7,456	$147.11	$154.17	$1,149,501	n/a
	1995	5,727	$142.98	$152.75	$874,772	n/a
	Missouri Averages			$131.28		n/a
South Dakota	1999	2,513	$55.36	$55.36	$139,120	8.60%
	1998	2,596	$49.42	$50.23	$130,410	8.80%
	1997	2,791	$45.53	$46.83	$130,691	8.70%
	1996	2,712	$46.40	$48.63	$131,877	8.80%
	1995	2,652	$51.15	$54.64	$144,914	9.10%
	South Dakota Averages:			$51.04		8.80%
total		454,283			$94,720,380	
avg win/unit/day all slots:			$208.51			

(cont. on next page)

source: Gaming Industry 1999 Statistical Abstract

	year	number of slots	win/unit/ day	win/unit/ day in 1999 dollars	win/unit/ day for all slots (1999 $)	slot hold
Reno, Nevada	2000	20,542	$81.53	$79.93	$1,641,889	4.94%
	1999	19,842	$78.45	$78.45	$1,556,605	4.95%
	1998	19,938	$74.71	$75.94	$1,514,129	4.90%
	1997	20,839	$68.38	$70.33	$1,465,524	4.90%
	1996	21,046	$65.51	$68.65	$1,444,902	4.86%
	Reno Averages			$74.58		4.91%
Sparks, Nevada	2000	5,243	$75.25	$73.77	$386,785	4.53%
	1999	5,490	$68.16	$68.16	$374,198	4.45%
	1998	5,432	$65.32	$66.40	$360,669	4.34%
	1997	5,232	$65.00	$66.85	$349,758	4.27%
	1996	5,161	$62.44	$65.44	$337,721	4.15%
	Sparks Averages			$68.12		4.35%
Win/Unit/Day all Reno/Sparks Slots				$73.25		4.79%

	year	number of slots	win/unit/ day	win/unit/ day in 1999 dollars	win/unit/ day for all slots (1999 $)	slot hold
Las Vegas, (Strip) Nevada	2000	61433	$106.18	$104.09	$6,394,816	6.02%
	1999	59999	$100.70	$100.70	$6,041,899	6.02%
	1998	55246	$96.15	$97.74	$5,399,490	5.92%
	1997	53460	$93.37	$96.03	$5,133,616	5.67%
	1996	52231	$92.34	$96.77	$5,054,515	5.53%
Las Vegas Strip Averages:				$99.25		5.84%

source: Nevada Gaming Control Board Revenue Reports, 1996-2000

APPENDIX B: DRIVE / DISTANCE RATIO
(fair share analysis)

The following investigation compares the tourists who arrive to Reno/Sparks via car, bus, RV or motorcycle. It covers the following markets: Metropolitan Sacramento; Stockton (San Joaquin County); Chico (Butte County); Modesto; San Francisco Bay Area (Sonoma, Napa, Solano, Marlin, Contra Costa, Alameda, San Mateo, Santo Clara, San Francisco Counties); Redding (Shasta County); Fresno (Fresno and Madera Counties); Monterey Bay (Monterey County); Oregon State; Los Angeles/Orange County; Metropolitan San Diego; Washington State; and British Columbia, Canada.

Visitors who drive to Reno/Sparks from these thirteen areas represent, over a ten-year period (1990-1999), 44% of the total tourists (RSCVA ES8, ES7, 4, 10, 45). Visitors who drive to Reno/Sparks from the Northern California locations listed above, over a ten-year period (1990-1999), represent 31.2% of the total tourists (ES8, ES7, 4, 10, 45).

Please refer to the following example as to the explanations of the methodology used for the analysis.

(1)	visitors	to reno:	4,867,084
		City	**1990**
(2)	population	Sacramento	1,515,082
(3)	% of	visitors from sac	7.00%
(4)	total	visitors from sac	340,696
(5)	arrive via	auto, bus, rv	96.00%
(6)	actual #	using auto,bus,rv	327,068
(7)		autual visitors%	6.72%
(8)		Pop/total pop	3.98%
(9)		Sacramento	1.6895
(10)	total pop	all areas	38,091,514

(1) This is an estimation of the total number of visitors to Reno (ES 7).

(2) Line two is the population of the respective area. For example, Sacramento had a population of 1,515,082 in 1990 (California Department of Finance, report E4).

(3) Line three is the percentage of visitors that come from the respective area. For example, according to the Reno/Sparks Conventions and Visitors Authority, seven percent of the visitors to Reno/Sparks came from Metropolitan Sacramento in 1990 (RSCVA 10).

(4) Line four is line 3 multiplied by line 1. It represents the total number of visitors to Reno/Sparks from Sacramento in 1990.

(5) Line five is the percentage of visitors from the respective area in the corresponding year that arrived via automobile, motorcycle, bus or RV to Reno/Sparks. Meaning, ninety-six percent of the visitors to Reno/Sparks from Sacramento used a car, motorcycle, bus or RV in 1990.

(6) Line six is line five multiplied by line four. Out of the 340,696 visitors from Sacramento to Reno/Sparks in 1990, 327,068 of them used a car, motorcycle, bus or RV to reach their destination.

(7) Line seven is the actual visitors from the respective area that used a car, motorcycle, bus, or RV to reach their final destination of Reno/Sparks. Although seven percent of Reno/Sparks' total visitors in 1990 came from Sacramento, most of them (6.72% out of 7%) used an automobile, motorcycle, bus, or RV. It is line six divided by line one.

(8) Before understanding line eight, please read the explanation regarding line ten. Line eight is the population of the respective city, in the corresponding year divided by the combined population of all thirteen areas in that same year. It is line two divided by line ten. For example, Sacramento had a population of 1,515,082 in 1990. The thirteen areas listed above had a population of 38,091,514 in 1990. Line two divided by line ten equals 3.98.

(9) Line nine is the end product of all work listed above. It is line seven divided by line eight.

(10) Line ten is the combined population of all thirteen areas listed above for the corresponding year.

Basically, line 9 tells us, in the above example, that Reno/Sparks has exceeded its fair share of driving tourists from Sacramento in 1990 by 68.95%:

3.98% x 1.6895 = 6.72%
line 8 x line 9 = line 7

Ten-year trends for the thirteen areas follow on the next pages (tables III-1 to III-6):

One would expect the cities most distant to Reno to have smaller drive/ distance ratios numbers. Although this generally occurs (Los Angeles, San Diego), it is not always the case (Oregon, Washington, British Columbia, Canada).

Also, besides California, a significant number of tourists come to Reno/Sparks from Washington State, Oregon and British Columbia, Canada. Casino gaming within these states has probably already diverted some potential Northern Nevada visitors.

Table III- 1 TEN YEAR TREND: FAIR SHARE ANALYSIS

(Sacramento, Stockton, Chico)

(1)	visitors to reno:	4,867,084	4,540,099	4,448,142	4,477,731	4,472,506	4,851,272	5,215,010	5,155,919	5,121,693	5,051,101
	city	1990	1991	1992	1993	1994	1995	1996	1997	1998	1999
(2)	population **Sacramento**	1,515,082	1,549,100	1,588,100	1,614,000	1,632,300	1,646,400	1,666,400	1,692,000	1,724,700	1,765,900
(3)	% of visitors from sac	7.0%	7.5%	7.6%	6.7%	7.0%	7.4%	8.9%	8.6%	8.9%	9.5%
(4)	total visitors from sac	340,696	340,507	338,059	300,008	313,075	358,994	464,136	443,409	455,831	479,855
(5)	arrive via auto, bus, rv	96%	95%	95%	94%	92%	94%	95%	97%	94%	92%
(6)	actual # using auto,bus,rv	327,068	323,482	321,156	282,007	288,029	337,454	440,929	430,107	428,481	441,466
(7)	autual visitors%	6.7200%	7.1250%	7.2200%	6.2980%	6.4400%	6.9560%	8.4550%	8.3420%	8.3660%	8.7400%
(8)	pop/total pop	3.9775%	4.0099%	4.0354%	4.0411%	4.0443%	4.0429%	4.0547%	4.0649%	4.0882%	4.1301%
(9)	Sacramento	1.6895	1.7769	1.7892	1.5585	1.5923	1.7206	2.0852	2.0522	2.0464	2.1162
(2)	population **Stockton**	495,277	501,900	511,700	518,000	522,200	528,200	534,800	541,500	548,800	557,700
(3)	% of visitors from	1.9%	2.2%	2.2%	1.7%	2.2%	2.2%	2.6%	2.5%	2.5%	2.5%
(4)	total visitors from	92,475	99,882	97,859	76,121	98,395	106,728	135,590	128,898	128,042	126,278
(5)	arrive via auto, bus, rv	96%	95%	95%	94%	92%	94%	95%	97%	94%	92%
(6)	actual # using auto,bus,rv	88,776	94,888	92,966	71,554	90,524	100,324	128,811	125,031	120,360	116,175
(7)	autual visitors%	1.8240%	2.0900%	2.0900%	1.5980%	2.0240%	2.0680%	2.4700%	2.4250%	2.3500%	2.3000%
(8)	pop/total pop	1.3002%	1.2992%	1.3002%	1.2970%	1.2939%	1.2970%	1.3013%	1.3009%	1.3009%	1.3043%
(9)	Stockton	1.4028	1.6087	1.6074	1.2321	1.5643	1.5944	1.8981	1.8641	1.8065	1.7633
(2)	population **Chico**	186,843	189,800	193,300	195,500	197,500	199,500	200,300	201,200	202,400	203,200
(3)	% of visitors from	1.40%	0.90%	1.10%	0.70%	1.30%	1.00%	1.00%	0.70%	1.00%	1.10%
(4)	total visitors from	68,139	40,861	48,930	31,344	58,143	48,513	52,150	36,091	51,217	55,562
(5)	arrive via auto,bus,rv	89%	87%	86%	84%	82%	84%	81%	85%	84%	86%
(6)	actual # using auto,bus,rv	60,644	35,549	42,079	26,329	47,677	40,751	42,242	30,678	43,022	47,783
(7)	acutal visitor%	1.2460%	0.7830%	0.9460%	0.5880%	1.0660%	0.8400%	0.8100%	0.5950%	0.8400%	0.9460%
(8)	pop/total pop	0.4905%	0.4913%	0.4912%	0.4895%	0.4893%	0.4899%	0.4874%	0.4834%	0.4798%	0.4752%
(9)	Chico	2.5402	1.5937	1.9260	1.2013	2.1784	1.7147	1.6620	1.2309	1.7508	1.9906
(10)	total pop all areas	38,091,514	38,631,888	39,354,645	39,939,794	40,360,138	40,723,645	41,098,250	41,624,659	42,186,787	42,757,115

Table III- 2 TEN YEAR TREND: FAIR SHARE ANALYSIS

(Modesto, SF Bay Area, Redding)

(1)	visitors to reno:	4,867,084	4,540,099	4,448,142	4,477,731	4,472,506	4,851,272	5,215,010	5,155,919	5,121,693	5,051,101
	city	1990	1991	1992	1993	1994	1995	1996	1997	1998	1999
(2)	population **Modesto**	380,819	390,800	402,100	410,400	416,400	420,500	424,400	429,800	435,600	442,600
(3)	% of visitors from	0.7%	1.0%	0.7%	0.7%	1.2%	1.0%	1.9%	1.5%	1.5%	1.2%
(4)	total visitors from	34,070	45,401	31,137	31,344	53,670	48,513	99,085	77,339	76,825	60,613
(5)	arrive via auto,but,rv	89%	87%	86%	84%	82%	84%	81%	85%	84%	86%
(6)	actual # using auto,bus,rv	30322	39499	26778	26329	44009	40751	80259	65738	64533	52127
(7)	actual visitor %	0.6230%	0.8700%	0.6020%	0.5880%	0.9840%	0.8400%	1.5390%	1.2750%	1.2600%	1.0320%
(8)	pop/total pop	0.9997%	1.0116%	1.0217%	1.0275%	1.0317%	1.0326%	1.0326%	1.0326%	1.0326%	1.0351%
(9)	Modesto	0.6232	0.8600	0.5892	0.5722	0.9538	0.8135	1.4903	1.2348	1.2203	0.9970
(2)	population **S F Bay Area**	6,162,862	6,199,900	6,277,700	6,355,700	6,407,100	6,431,400	6,469,000	6,552,100	6,655,000	6,746,400
(3)	% of visitors from SF	19.5%	18.6%	18.7%	17.5%	20.0%	19.4%	19.9%	21.0%	19.8%	21.2%
(4)	total visitors from SF	949,081	844,458	831,803	783,603	894,501	941,147	1,037,787	1,082,743	1,014,095	1,070,833
(5)	arrive via auto, bus, rv	89%	87%	87%	85%	81%	84%	81%	85%	84%	83%
(6)	actual # using auto,bus,rv	844,682	734,679	723,668	666,062	724,546	790,563	840,607	920,332	851,840	888,792
(7)	actual visitors%	17.3550%	16.1820%	16.2690%	14.8750%	16.2000%	16.2960%	16.1190%	17.8500%	16.6320%	17.5960%
(8)	pop/total pop	16.1791%	16.0487%	15.9516%	15.9132%	15.8748%	15.7928%	15.7403%	15.7409%	15.7751%	15.7784%
(9)	SF	1.0727	1.0083	1.0199	0.9348	1.0205	1.0319	1.0241	1.1340	1.0543	1.1152
(2)	population **Redding**	150,146	153,800	157,900	159,800	160,800	161,400	161,700	162,300	163,200	163,500
(3)	% of visitors from	1.1%	1.1%	0.8%	0.8%	0.7%	1.1%	0.9%	1.1%	1.2%	1.0%
(4)	total visitors from	53,538	49,941	35,585	35,822	31,308	53,364	46,935	56,715	61,460	50,511
(5)	arrive via auto, bus,rv	89%	87%	86%	84%	82%	84%	81%	85%	84%	86%
(6)	actual # using auto,bus,rv	47,649	43,449	30,603	30,090	25,672	44,826	38,017	48,208	51,627	43,439
(7)	actual visitors%	0.9790%	0.9570%	0.6880%	0.6720%	0.5740%	0.9240%	0.7290%	0.9350%	1.0080%	0.8600%
(8)	pop/total pop	0.3942%	0.3981%	0.4012%	0.4001%	0.3984%	0.3963%	0.3934%	0.3899%	0.3869%	0.3824%
(9)	Redding	2.4837	2.4038	1.7148	1.6796	1.4407	2.3314	1.8529	2.3980	2.6057	2.2490
(10)	total pop all areas	38,091,514	38,631,888	39,354,645	39,939,794	40,360,138	40,723,645	41,098,250	41,624,659	42,186,787	42,757,115

Table III- 3 TEN YEAR TREND: FAIR SHARE ANALYSIS

(Fresno, Monterey, Oregon)

		1990	1991	1992	1993	1994	1995	1996	1997	1998	1999
(1)	visitors to reno:	4,867,084	4,540,099	4,448,142	4,477,731	4,472,506	4,851,272	5,215,010	5,155,919	5,121,693	5,051,101
	area	1990	1991	1992	1993	1994	1995	1996	1997	1998	1999
(2)	population **Fresno**	783,449	801,300	828,500	849,400	864,000	877,500	891,400	903,600	912,800	922,100
(3)	% of visitors from	1.5%	1.3%	1.7%	0.8%	1.3%	1.3%	0.9%	1.3%	1.4%	2.1%
(4)	total visitors from	73,006	59,021	75,618	35,822	58,143	63,067	46,935	67,027	71,704	106,073
(5)	arrive via auto,bus,rv	89%	87%	86%	84%	82%	84%	81%	85%	84%	86%
(6)	actual # using auto,bus,rv	64,976	51,349	65,032	30,090	47,677	52,976	38,017	56,973	60,231	91,223
(7)	actual visitor %	1.3350%	1.1310%	1.4620%	0.6720%	1.0660%	1.0920%	0.7290%	1.1050%	1.1760%	1.8060%
(8)	pop/total pop	2.0568%	2.0742%	2.1052%	2.1267%	2.1407%	2.1548%	2.1689%	2.1708%	2.1637%	2.1566%
(9)	Fresno	0.6491	0.5453	0.6945	0.3160	0.4980	0.5068	0.3361	0.5090	0.5435	0.8374
(2)	population **Monterey**	367,820	372,900	380,000	382,800	375,900	368,900	368,500	377,600	390,300	397,700
(3)	% Visitors from	1.70%	1.50%	1.30%	1.10%	1.40%	1.50%	1.10%	1.70%	1.50%	2.00%
(4)	total Visitors from	82,740	68,101	57,826	49,255	62,615	72,769	57,365	87,651	76,825	101,022
(5)	arrive via auto,bus,rv	89%	87%	86%	84%	82%	84%	81%	85%	84%	86%
(6)	actual # using auto,bus,rv	73,639	59,248	49,730	41,374	51,344	61,126	46,466	74,503	64,533	86,879
(7)	acutal visitors%	1.5130%	1.3050%	1.1180%	0.9240%	1.1480%	1.2600%	0.8910%	1.4450%	1.2600%	1.7200%
(8)	pop/total pop	0.9656%	0.9653%	0.9656%	0.9584%	0.9314%	0.9059%	0.8966%	0.9072%	0.9252%	0.9301%
(9)	Monterey	1.5669	1.3520	1.1579	0.9641	1.2326	1.3909	0.9937	1.5929	1.3619	1.8492
(2)	population **Oregon**	2,858,547	2,918,745	2,973,934	3,034,490	3,087,142	3,141,421	3,195,087	3,243,254	3,282,055	3,316,154
(3)	% of visitors from	9.00%	9.40%	8.70%	8.80%	7.80%	7.10%	9.10%	7.00%	7.20%	7.00%
(4)	total visitors from	438,038	426,769	386,988	394,040	348,855	344,440	474,566	360,914	368,762	353,577
(5)	arrive via auto,bus,rv	67%	73%	78%	67%	55%	58%	48%	64%	62%	58%
(6)	actual # using auto,bus,rv	293,485	311,542	301,851	264,007	191,871	199,775	227,792	230,985	228,632	205,075
(7)	actual visitor %	6.03%	6.86%	6.79%	5.90%	4.29%	4.12%	4.37%	4.48%	4.46%	4.06%
(8)	pop/total pop	7.50%	7.56%	7.56%	7.60%	7.65%	7.71%	7.77%	7.79%	7.78%	7.76%
(9)	Oregon	0.803527	0.908240	0.898005	0.776028	0.560659	0.533835	0.561854	0.574973	0.573792	0.523480
(10)	total pop all areas	38,091,514	38,631,888	39,354,645	39,939,794	40,360,138	40,723,645	41,098,250	41,624,659	42,186,787	42,757,115

Table III- 4 TEN YEAR TREND: FAIR SHARE ANALYSIS

(LA/Orange, San Diego, Washington)

(1)	visitors to reno:	4,867,084	4,540,099	4,448,142	4,477,731	4,472,506	4,851,272	5,215,010	5,155,919	5,121,693	5,051,101
	area	1990	1991	1992	1993	1994	1995	1996	1997	1998	1999
(2)	Population **LA/Orange**	14,968,902	15,121,900	15,363,500	15,524,100	15,604,200	15,657,500	15,718,600	15,856,800	16,043,500	16,273,900
(3)	% of visitors from	5.0%	3.9%	4.3%	5.9%	3.3%	3.3%	3.2%	3.7%	4.0%	2.8%
(4)	total visitors from	243,354	177,064	191,270	264,186	147,593	160,092	166,880	190,769	204,868	141,431
(5)	arrive via auto,bus,rv	9.0%	6.9%	11.0%	13.0%	15.0%	10.0%	2.0%	7.0%	6.0%	14.0%
(6)	actual # using auto,bus,rv	21,902	12,217	21,040	34,344	22,139	16,009	3,338	13,354	12,292	19,800
(7)	acutal visitor %	0.45%	0.27%	0.47%	0.77%	0.50%	0.33%	0.06%	0.26%	0.24%	0.39%
(8)	pop/total pop	39.3%	39.1%	39.0%	38.9%	38.7%	38.4%	38.2%	38.1%	38.0%	38.1%
(9)	LA	0.01145	0.00687	0.01212	0.01973	0.01280	0.00858	0.00167	0.00680	0.00631	0.01030
(2)	population **San Diego**	2,560,552	2,589,500	2,628,600	2,646,600	2,653,100	2,657,800	2,662,200	2,692,800	2,741,900	2,789,600
(3)	% of visitors from	0.60%	0.90%	0.60%	1.20%	0.80%	0.80%	0.60%	0.40%	0.50%	0.40%
(4)	total visitors from	29203	40861	26689	53733	35780	38810	31290	20624	25608	20204
(5)	arrive via auto,bus,rv	15.0%	12.0%	11.0%	13.0%	17.0%	11.0%	6.0%	11.0%	10.0%	8.0%
(6)	actual # using auto,bus,rv	4380	4903	2936	6985	6083	4269	1877	2269	2561	1616
(7)	actual visitor %	0.09%	0.11%	0.07%	0.16%	0.14%	0.09%	0.04%	0.04%	0.05%	0.03%
(8)	pop/total pop	6.72%	6.70%	6.68%	6.63%	6.57%	6.53%	6.48%	6.47%	6.50%	6.52%
(9)	SD	0.01339	0.01611	0.00988	0.02354	0.02069	0.01348	0.00556	0.00680	0.00769	0.00490
(2)	population **Washington**	4,900,780	5,013,443	5,139,011	5,247,704	5,334,896	5,431,024	5,509,963	5,604,105	5,687,832	5,756,361
(3)	% of visitors from	11.3%	9.8%	10.9%	11.6%	13.2%	11.6%	11.0%	10.3%	9.5%	10.2%
(4)	total visitors from	549,980	444,930	484,847	519,417	590,371	562,748	573,651	531,060	486,561	515,212
(5)	arrive via auto,bus,rv	44%	56%	54%	41%	26%	36%	21%	27%	37%	28%
(6)	actual # using auto,bus,rv	241,991	249,161	261,818	212,961	153,496	202,589	120,467	143,386	180,028	144,259
(7)	actual visitor %	4.9720%	5.4880%	5.8860%	4.7560%	3.4320%	4.1760%	2.3100%	2.7810%	3.5150%	2.8560%
(8)	pop/total pop	12.8658%	12.9775%	13.0582%	13.1390%	13.2182%	13.3363%	13.4068%	13.4634%	13.4825%	13.4629%
(9)	Washington	0.38645	0.42289	0.45075	0.36197	0.25964	0.31313	0.17230	0.20656	0.26071	0.21214
(10)	total pop all areas	38,091,514	38,631,888	39,354,645	39,939,794	40,360,138	40,723,645	41,098,250	41,624,659	42,186,787	42,757,115

Table III- 5 TEN YEAR TREND: FAIR SHARE ANALYSIS
(BC, Canada)

(1)	visitors	to reno:	4,867,084	4,540,099	. 4,448,142	4,477,731	4,472,506	4,851,272	5,215,010	5,155,919	5,121,693	5,051,101
		area	1990	1991	1992	1993	1994	1995	1996	1997	1998	1999
(2)	population	BC, Canada	3,291,400	3,373,400	3,470,300	3,571,500	3,681,800	3,784,000	3,882,000	3,959,700	3,997,500	4,028,100
(3)	% of	visitors from	7.50%	9.60%	7.50%	7.00%	7.20%	6.00%	6.60%	6.00%	3.80%	3.70%
(4)	total	visitors from	365,031	435,850	333,611	313,441	322,020	291,076	344,191	309,355	194,624	186,891
(5)	arrive via	auto,bus,rv	45%	53%	41%	45%	52%	47%	50%	56%	47%	58%
(6)	actual #	using auto,bus,rv	164,264	231,000	136,780	141,049	167,451	136,806	172,095	173,239	91,473	108,397
(7)		actual visitor %	3.37500%	5.08800%	3.07500%	3.15000%	3.74400%	2.82000%	3.30000%	3.36000%	1.78600%	2.14600%
(8)		pop/total pop	8.64077%	8.73216%	8.81802%	8.94221%	9.12237%	9.29190%	9.44566%	9.51287%	9.47572%	9.42089%
(9)		BC	0.39059	0.58267	0.34872	0.35226	0.41042	0.30349	0.34937	0.35321	0.18848	0.22779
(10)	total pop	all areas	38,091,514	38,631,888	39,354,645	39,939,794	40,360,138	40,723,645	41,098,250	41,624,659	42,186,787	42,757,115

Table III- 6 ten year trend: fair share analysis all thirteen areas

miles fr reno	city	1990	1991	1992	1993	1994	1995	1996	1997	1998	1999	avg
134	Sacramento	1.68951	1.77685	1.78919	1.55849	1.59235	1.72056	2.08525	2.05220	2.04635	2.11619	1.84269
165	Chico	2.54021	1.59372	1.92600	1.20126	2.17843	1.71468	1.66199	1.23095	1.75084	1.99056	1.77886
179	Stockton	1.40283	1.60870	1.60741	1.23212	1.56432	1.59441	1.89814	1.86408	1.80647	1.76334	1.63418
204	Modesto	0.62316	0.86002	0.58919	0.57224	0.95376	0.81350	1.49034	1.23479	1.22028	0.99696	0.93542
217	SF	1.07268	1.00831	1.01990	0.93476	1.02048	1.03186	1.02406	1.13399	1.05432	1.11519	1.04158
217	Redding	2.48369	2.40382	1.71476	1.67957	1.44072	2.33139	1.85285	2.39797	2.60565	2.24900	2.11594
300	Fresno	0.64908	0.54527	0.69447	0.31598	0.49796	0.50678	0.33611	0.50902	0.54351	0.83743	0.54356
316	Monterey	1.56687	1.35196	1.15786	0.96406	1.23260	1.39094	0.99372	1.59289	1.36191	1.84919	1.34620
426	Oregon	0.80353	0.90824	0.89800	0.77603	0.56086	0.53383	0.56185	0.57497	0.57379	0.52348	0.67146
515	LA	0.01145	0.00687	0.01212	0.01973	0.01280	0.00858	0.00167	0.00680	0.00631	0.01030	0.00966
635	SD	0.01339	0.01611	0.00988	0.02354	0.02069	0.01348	0.00556	0.00680	0.00769	0.00490	0.01221
659	Washington	0.38645	0.42289	0.45075	0.36197	0.25964	0.31313	0.17230	0.20656	0.26071	0.21214	0.30465
1393	BC, Canada	0.39059	0.58267	0.34872	0.35226	0.41042	0.30349	0.34937	0.35321	0.18848	0.22779	0.35070

APPENDIX C: SUPPLEMENTS TO V-3, V-4, V-5

Sacramento & Stockton	Year	% Drive to Reno	X	% Total Visitors	X	% Gamble?	=	Potential Lost Gaming Visitor
	1999	92%		12.00%		91%		10.05%
	1998	94%		11.40%		90%		9.64%
	1997	97%		11.10%		92%		9.91%
	1996	95%		11.50%		92%		10.05%
	1995	94%		9.60%		92%		8.30%
	1994	92%		9.20%		92%		7.79%
	1993	94%		7.80%		91%		6.67%
	1992	95%		9.80%		94%		8.75%
	1991	95%		9.70%		94%		8.66%
	1990	96%		8.90%		95%		8.12%
10 year average		94.40%		10.10%		92.30%		8.79%

SF Bay Area	Year	% Drive to Reno	X	% Total Visitors	X	% Gamble?	=	Potential Lost Gaming Visitor
	1999	83%		21.20%		91%		16.01%
	1998	84%		19.80%		90%		14.97%
	1997	85%		21.00%		92%		16.42%
	1996	81%		19.90%		92%		14.83%
	1995	84%		19.40%		92%		14.99%
	1994	81%		20.00%		92%		14.90%
	1993	85%		17.50%		91%		13.54%
	1992	87%		18.70%		94%		15.29%
	1991	87%		18.60%		94%		15.21%
	1990	89%		19.50%		95%		16.49%
10 year average		84.60%		19.56%		92.30%		15.27%

OTHER N. CA	Year	% Drive to Reno	X	% Total Visitors	X	% Gamble?	=	Potential Lost Gaming Visitor
	1999	86%		11.10%		91%		8.69%
	1998	84%		10.30%		90%		7.79%
	1997	85%		10.70%		92%		8.37%
	1996	81%		9.80%		92%		7.30%
	1995	84%		9.90%		92%		7.65%
	1994	82%		10.50%		92%		7.92%
	1993	84%		8.00%		91%		6.12%
	1992	86%		9.50%		94%		7.68%
	1991	87%		8.30%		94%		6.79%
	1990	89%		9.20%		91%		7.45%
10 year average		84.80%		9.73%		91.90%		7.57%

source: RSCVA 1999 Final Report

Table V-1

Win/Slot/Day, Non-Nevada Locations

V-1(a)

	five year trend: win/ unit/ day (IN 1999 $)	five year trend: hold percentage
Atlantic City	$234.84	8.37%
Colorado	$92.45	5.87%
Connecticut	$372.49	n/a
Delaware	$327.89	n/a
Illinois	$302.03	n/a
Indiana	$222.69	n/a
Iowa	$157.19	n/a
Missouri	$131.28	n/a
South Dakota	$51.04	8.80%
avg all non-NV casinos:	$208.51	

Sources:
Appendix A
Nevada Gaming Revenue Report (1996-2000)

Win/Slot/Day, Reno, Sparks, LV Strip, Nevada

V-1(b)

	five year trend: win/ unit/ day (IN 1999 $)	five year trend: hold percentage
Reno,NV	$74.58	4.91%
Sparks, NV	$68.12	4.35%
avg Reno/Sparks:	$73.25	4.79%
LV Strip, NV	$99.25	5.84%

TABLE V-2
Estimates of Win / Unit / Day for Reno/Sparks 8 major competitors
(IN 1999 DOLLARS)

Category	Reno	Las Vegas Strip	low estimate	avg of all non NV Casinos	Connecticut	high estimate
Win/Unit/Day	$73.25	$99.25	$200.00	$208.51	$372.49	$500.00
Slot Revenue	$855,573,172	$1,159,207,449	$2,336,000,000	$2,435,396,800	$4,350,683,200	$5,840,000,000
Est Table Revenue	$284,905,866	$386,016,081	$777,888,000	$810,987,134	$1,448,777,506	$1,944,720,000
total	$1,140,479,038	$1,545,223,530	$3,113,888,000	$3,246,383,934	$5,799,460,706	$7,784,720,000
Est Net Income	$433,382,035	$587,184,941	$1,183,277,440	$1,233,625,895	$2,203,795,068	$2,958,193,600

sources: Gaming Industry 1999 Statistical Abstract
Nevada Gaming Abstracts 1996-2000
General Accounting Office Report GGD 97-91 (May 1997)

TABLE V-3
10 Year trend, Northern California Visitor to Reno/Sparks

	% Drive to Reno	X	% Total Visitors	X	% Gamble?	=	Potential Lost Gaming Visitor
Sacramento/Stockton	94.40%		10.10%		92.30%		8.79%
SF Bay Area	84.60%		19.56%		92.30%		15.27%
Other N CA	84.80%		9.73%		92.30%		7.57%
							31.63%

source: Appendix A
RSCVA 1999 Final Report

Graph V-4: Forecasted Visitors to Reno/Sparks Based on a Simple Linear Regression

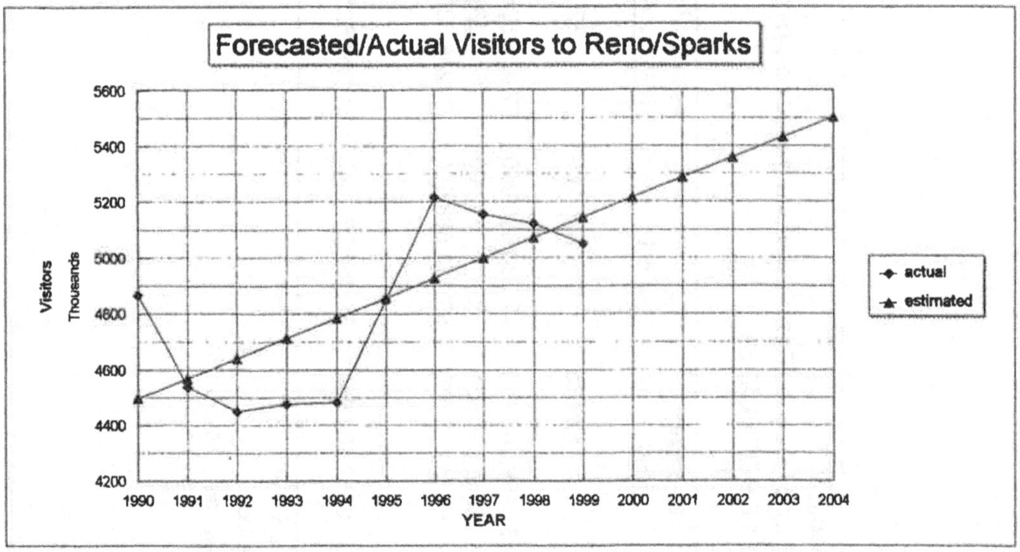

source: RSCVA 1999 Final Report

year	actual	estimated
2004		5,503,144
2003		5,431,345
2002		5,359,547
2001		5,287,748
2000		5,215,949
1999	5,051,101	5,144,150
1998	5,121,693	5,072,351
1997	5,155,919	5,000,553
1996	5,215,010	4,928,754
1995	4,851,272	4,856,955
1994	4,482,506	4,785,156
1993	4,477,731	4,713,358
1992	4,448,142	4,641,559
1991	4,540,099	4,569,760
1990	4,867,084	4,497,961

Regression Output:		
Constant		4,497,961
Std Err of Y Est		234218.1
R Squared		0.492147
No. of Observations		10
Degrees of Freedom		8
X Coefficient(s)	71,799	
Std Err of Coef.	25787	
	2.784	

Table V-5: Estimated Loss in Reno/Sparks Gaming Visitors

Forecasted Visitors 2004: 5,503,144

	Percentage	Total Visitors	% who list gaming as primary trip purpose	Potential Total Loss in Gaming Visitors	Estimated Diversion of Gaming Visitors	Estimated Loss in Gaming Visitors	Avg Stay (Days)
SF Bay Area	15.27%	840,090	80.20%	673,752	56.95%	383,702	1.9
Sac/Stockton	8.79%	483,940	79.30%	383,764	56.95%	218,554	1.6
Other N CA	7.57%	416,862	77.90%	324,735	56.95%	184,937	1.8
		1,740,892		1,382,252		787,193	

Amount Spent Per Day

City/Area	Gaming	F&B	Hotel	Retail	Shows	Sightseeing	Recreation	Special Events
SF Bay Area	$247.00	$33.71	$26.10	$24.79	$7.21	$3.43	$2.01	$1.42
Sac/Stockton	$181.00	$33.71	$26.10	$24.79	$7.21	$3.43	$2.01	$1.42
Other N CA	$196.00	$33.71	$26.10	$24.79	$7.21	$3.43	$2.01	$1.42

sources: RSCVA Final Reoprt
Appendix C
Graph V-4

Table V-5b: Estimated Loss in Reno/Sparks Revenues

Amount Spent Per Person Per Trip

City/Area	Gaming	F&B	Hotel	Retail	Shows	Sightseeing	Recreation	Special Events
SF Bay Area	$469.30	$64.05	$49.59	$47.11	$13.70	$6.52	$3.82	$2.70
Sac/Stockton	$289.60	$53.94	$41.76	$39.67	$11.53	$5.49	$3.21	$2.27
Other N CA	$352.80	$60.68	$46.98	$44.63	$12.97	$6.18	$3.62	$2.55

Amount Spent for All Visitors Forecasted from N CA

City/Area	Gaming	F&B	Hotel	Retail	Shows	Sightseeing	Recreation	Special Events
SF Bay Area	$180,071,323	$24,576,490	$19,026,721	$18,074,571	$5,254,909	$2,502,503	$1,464,297	$1,034,429
Sac/Stockton	$63,293,191	$11,788,286	$9,126,301	$8,669,595	$2,520,554	$1,200,343	$702,361	$496,171
Other N CA	$36,247,612	$6,234,413	$4,826,582	$4,585,046	$1,333,033	$634,820	$371,454	$262,408
totals	$279,612,126	$42,599,190	$32,979,603	$31,329,212	$9,108,497	$4,337,666	$2,538,112	$1,793,007

sources: RSCVA, 2000 Final Report

TABLE V-6

PERCENTAGE OF DISPOSABLE INCOME SPENT ON GAMBLING: CA, US, OR

CALIFORNIA		
1995 CA population	31,600,000	
per capita disposable income	$20,971	
total disposable income	$662,683,600,000	
gambling spend		%
California	$2,500,000,000	0.3773%
Nevada	$2,592,203,950	0.3912%
total	$5,092,203,950	
% of disposable income spent on gaming:	0.7684%	

sources: us census
Dunstan, gambling in CA
Nevada Gaming Abstract
Ader, Falcone, Steinberg
BEA

UNITED STATES	
1999 US population	272,690,813
per capita disposable income	$24,297
total disposable income	$6,625,568,683,461
gambling spend	
US	$58,260,500,000
% of disposable income spent on gaming:	0.8793%

sources: us census
NGISC
BEA

OREGON	
1998 OR Population	3,282,055
per capita disposable income	$21,927
total disposable income	$71,965,619,985
per capita disposable income spent on gaming:	$282
total disposable income spent on gaming:	$925,539,510
% of disposable income spent on gaming:	1.2861%

sources: us census
BEA
Gambling Magazine

TABLE V-7

CALCULATION OF EXPECTED DIVERSION DUE TO NORTHERN CALIFORNIA TRIBAL CASINOS

California spent on Casino Gambling in 1999:

Per Capita DI	$25,100	x
California Population	33,145,121	x
% of DI spent on gaming	0.3912%	=
	$3,254,559,205	

If California mimics the percentage of Disposable Income Oregon Spends on Casino Gambling

(Population and Per Capita Disposable Income in 1999 figures)

Per Capita DI	$25,100	x
California Population	33,145,121	x
% DI spent on gaming	0.9088%	=
CA casino gaming mkt.	**$7,560,693,777**	

If California Substitutes this % of Casino gaming in their own state for Nevada Casino Gaming	then Nevada earns this revenue from California
0.00%	$7,560,693,777
10.00%	$6,804,624,399
20.00%	$6,048,555,022
30.00%	$5,292,485,644
40.00%	$4,536,416,266
50.00%	$3,780,346,889
56.95%	**$3,254,559,202**
60.00%	$3,024,277,511
70.00%	$2,268,208,133
80.00%	$1,512,138,755
90.00%	$756,069,378
100.00%	$0

sources: Ader, Falcone, Steinberg
U. S. Census
BEA

TABLE V-8

Forecasted Loss in Gaming (and Associated Revenues) According to Overall Diversion Rate

Diversion Rate	Gaming	F&B	Hotel	Retail	Shows	Sightseeing	Recreation	Special Events
0.00%	-	-	-	-	-	-	-	-
10.00%	$49,097,827	$7,480,104	$5,790,975	$5,501,179	$1,599,385	$761,662	$445,674	$314,839
20.00%	$98,195,654	$14,960,208	$11,581,950	$11,002,358	$3,198,770	$1,523,324	$891,348	$629,678
30.00%	$147,293,481	$22,440,312	$17,372,925	$16,503,537	$4,798,155	$2,284,986	$1,337,022	$944,517
40.00%	$196,391,308	$29,920,416	$23,163,900	$22,004,716	$6,397,540	$3,046,648	$1,782,696	$1,259,356
50.00%	$245,489,135	$37,400,520	$28,954,875	$27,505,895	$7,996,925	$3,808,310	$2,228,370	$1,574,195
60.00%	$294,586,962	$44,880,624	$34,745,850	$33,007,074	$9,596,310	$4,569,972	$2,674,044	$1,889,034
70.00%	$343,684,789	$52,360,728	$40,536,825	$38,508,253	$11,195,695	$5,331,634	$3,119,718	$2,203,873
80.00%	$392,782,616	$59,840,832	$46,327,800	$44,009,432	$12,795,080	$6,093,296	$3,565,392	$2,518,712
90.00%	$441,880,443	$67,320,936	$52,118,775	$49,510,611	$14,394,465	$6,854,958	$4,011,066	$2,833,551
100.00%	$490,978,270	$74,801,040	$57,909,750	$55,011,790	$15,993,850	$7,616,620	$4,456,740	$3,148,390

TABLE/GRAPH V-9

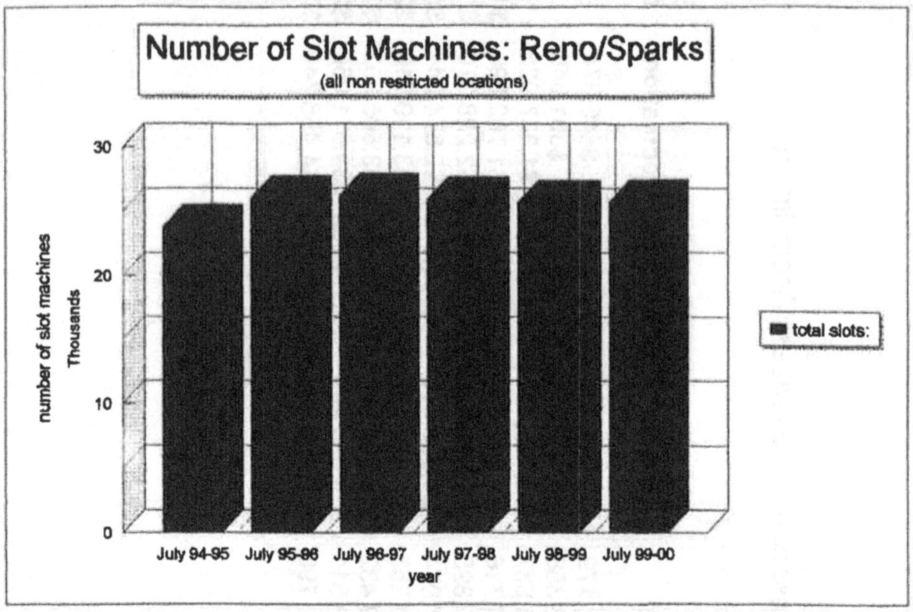

Time Frame	July 94-95	July 95-96	July 96-97	July 97-98	July 98-99	July 99-00
total slots:	23,721	26,004	26,150	25,851	25,606	25,689

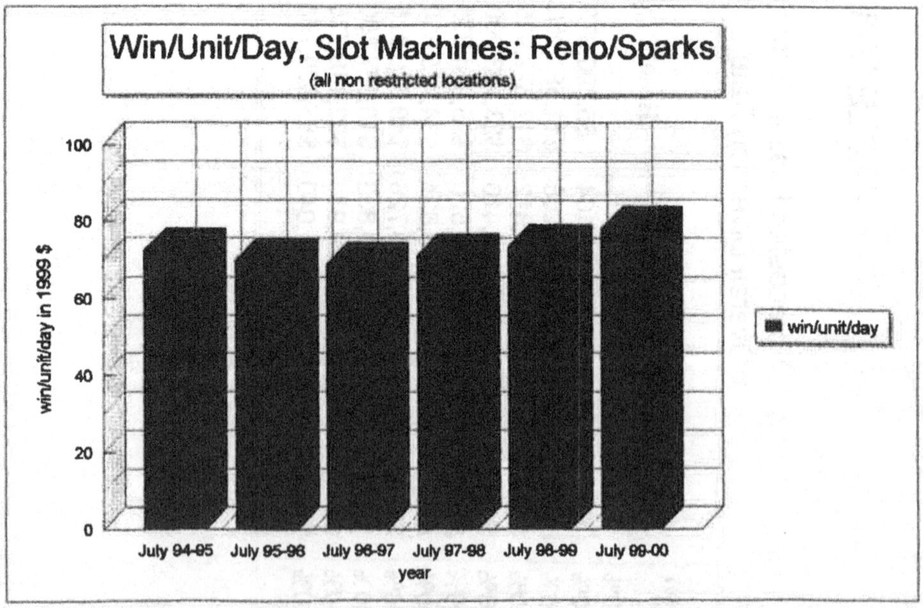

Time Frame	July 94-95	July 95-96	July 96-97	July 97-98	July 98-99	July 99-00
win/unit/day	$72.47	$69.89	$68.89	$71.12	$73.58	$78.17

source: Nevada Gaming revenue Reports, 1995-2000

GRAPH V-10

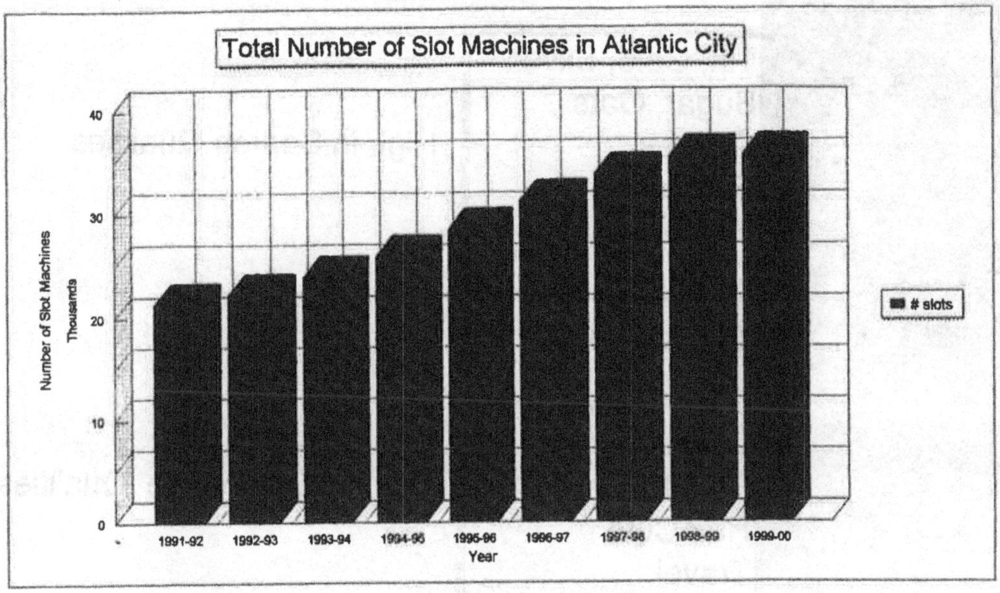

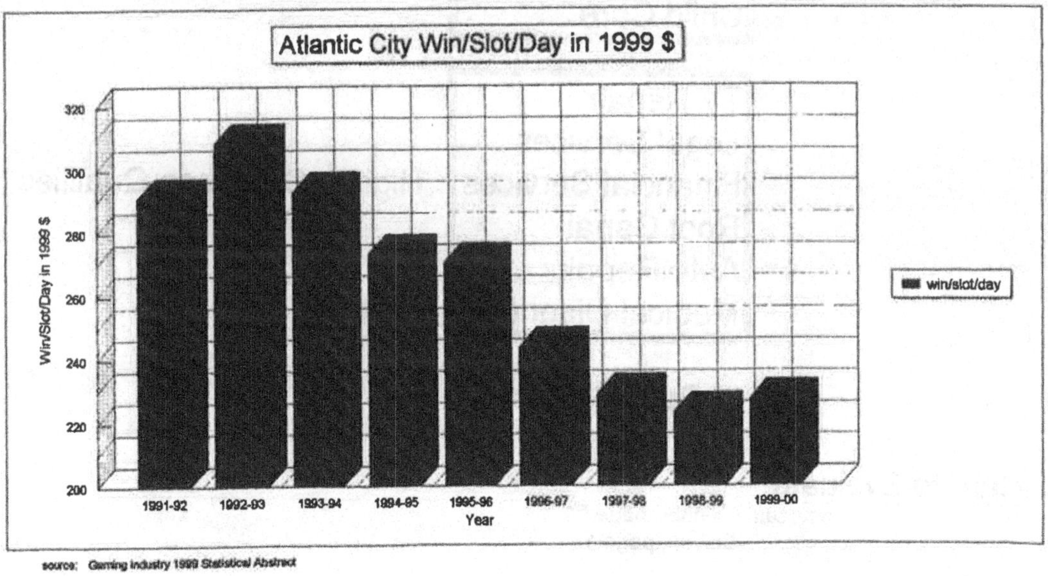

source: *Gaming Industry 1999 Statistical Abstract*

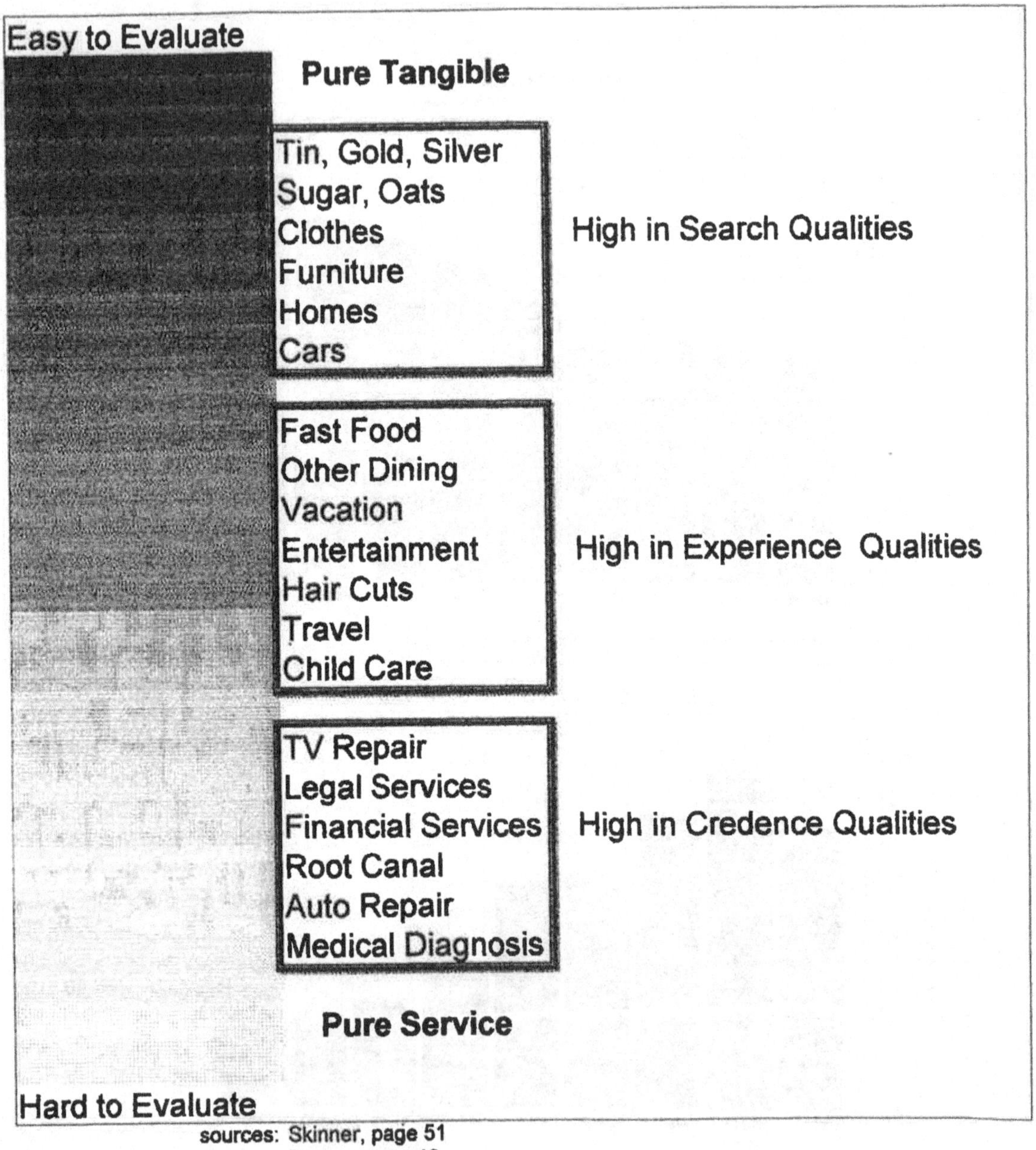

sources: Skinner, page 51
Bowen, page 18

Work Cited

Ader, Jason, Marc Falcone, and Adam Steinberg. "Native American Gaming in California: Nevada's Biggest Risk?" Bear Stearns, February 2000.

Aguayo, Rafael. The American Who Taught the Japanese About Quality. New York: Simon & Schuster, 1990.

Albrecht, Karl and Ron Zemke. Service America! Doing Business in the New Economy. Homewood: Dow Jones-Irwin, 1985.

Arendt, Klaus and Rudi Hartmann. Casino Gambling in America: Origins, Trends, and Impacts. New York: Cognizant Communications Corporation, 1998.

Benedict, Jeff. Without Reservation. New York: Harper Collins, 2000.

Bossong, Eileen, ed. "Lodging and Gaming Industry Survey." New York: Standard and Poor, February 2001.

Bowen, John, ed. Hospitality Marketing Today. Dubuque: Kendall Hunt, 1994.

California Demographics. California State Department of Finance. 10 December 2001. <http://www.dof.ca.gov/HTML/DEMOGRAP/druhpar.htm>.

Christiansen, Eugene and Sebastian Sinclair. "Gross Annual Wager of the United States-2000." CCA-I.COM. 7 January 2002. <http://www.cca-i.com>.

"Most Indians haven't Benefited from the 1990s Casino boom, Analysis Shows." Cable News Network and Associated Press. 12 December 2001. <http://www.cnn.com/2000/US/08/31/indian.gambling.ap/>.

Cole, David. "Thompson Won't Oppose Dairyland Casino," Milwaukee J. Sentinel 30 August 1999.

Cornell, Stephen, and Jonathan Taylor. "An Analysis of the Economic Impacts of Indian Gaming in the State of Arizona." Udall Center for Studies of Public Policy. Tucson: June 2001.

Curtis, Harry and Smedes Rose. "Tribal Gaming in California." Robertson Stephens. New York: 29 December 1999.

Cummings, Will. "The Revenue Performance and Impacts of Arizona's Native American Casinos." Cummings Associates. Arlington: February 2001.

Desiderio, Denise (National Indian Gaming Commission) Personal Interview. 7 September 2001.

DeSilva, Cynthia. "Waging the Wager War: Tribal Sovereignty, Tribal Gaming and California's Proposition 5 and Chapter 409." McGeorge Law Review. Spring 1999: 1-73.

Disposable Income Time Series. Bureau of Economic Affairs. 1 January 2002. http://www. Bea.doc.gov/bea/regional/articles/0600spi/TAB3C.htm

Dunstan, Roger. "The Evolution and Impact of Indian Gambling in California" Gambling Law Review. 5-4 (2001): 373-382.

---. "Gambling in California" California Research Bureau. Sacramento: CRB, January 1997.

Eadington, William R. "The Economics of Casino Gambling" Journal of Economic Perspectives 13.3 (Summer 1999): 179-192

---, ed. Indian Gaming and the Law. Reno: Institute for the Study of Gambling and Commercial Gaming, 1998.

---, Personal interview. 12 December 2001.

Eisler, Kim. Revenge of the Pequots. New York: Simon & Schuster, 2001.

Fragan, S. "Indian Bingo Showdown" The Washington Monthly, 17-4 (1985): 34-38.

Gallegos, Gilbert. "Pojoaque, Mescaleros won't join casino deal." Albuquerque Tribune (WWW.ABQTRIB.COM) 22 November 2001.

---, "Pojoaque Leader Vows to Continue Court Fight Over Gambling." Albuquerque Tribune (WWW.ABQTRIB.COM) 29 November 2001.

"Gambling in Oregon" State of Oregon. 2 November 2001 http://www.governor.state.or.us/governor/gambl.htm

Gambling Magazine. Oregonians Set Record Gambling High. 30 December 2001. http://www.gamblingmagazine.com/articles/42/42-30.htm

Hashimoto, Kathryn, Sheryl Kline, and George Fenich, ed. Casino Management Past Present Future. Dubuque: Kendall Hunt Publishing, 1998.

International Gaming Institute, University of Nevada, Las Vegas. The Gaming Industry, Introduction and Perspectives. New York: Wiley & Sons, 1996.

Jackson, Andrew, Microsoft Encarta Online Encyclopedia 2001. http://encarta.msn.com. 1997-2000 Microsoft Corporation.

Johnson, Wendy. "Tribal Gaming Expansion in Oregon." Willamette Law Review. Spring 2001: Lexis1-40.

Jorgensen, Miriam and Johathan Taylor. What determines Indian Economic Success? Evidence from tribal and Individual Indian Enterprises-PRS0003. Boston: Harvard University, Project on American Indian Development, June 2000.

Kelly, Joseph. "Indian Gaming Law." Drake Law Review Volume 43 (1993-1994): 501-545.

Kilby, Jim and Jim Fox. Casino Operations Management. New York: John Wiley & Sons, 1998.

Light, Steven and Kathryn Rand. "Are all Bets Off? Off Reservation Indians gambling in Wisconsin." Gambling Law Review 5-4 (2001): 351-372.

Hill, Barry, comp. Casino Gaming Regulation: Roles of Five States and the National Indian Gaming Commission-RCED-98-97. Washington DC: GAO, 5-1998.

Leupp, John and Gregg Klein. Gaming Industry 1999 Statistical Abstract. New York: Donaldson, Lufkin & Jenrette, February 2000.

Leupp, John and Joo Eun Lee. Gaming Industry 1999 Statistical Abstract. New York: Donaldson, Lufkin & Jenrette, February 2000.

Mapquest. December 2001. Mapquest.com, Incorporated. 11 December 2001 <http:// www.Mapquest.com>

Marshall, John (jurist), Microsoft Encarta Online Encyclopedia. 2001. <http://encarta.msn.com.1997-2000>Microsoft Corporation.

Mason, Dale. Indian Gaming Tribal Sovereignty and American Politics. Norman: University of Oklahoma Press, 2000.

Merriam-Webster Online, The Language Center. Merriam-Webster Incorporated. 10 December 2001. <http://www.M-W.com>

Meyer-Arendt, Klaus and Rudi Hartmann, ed. Casino Gambling in America: Orgins, Trends, and Impacts. New York: Cognizant Communication Corporation. 1998.

Morain, Dan. "Card Clubs Fight Tribal Gaming." Sacramento Times 17 November 2001.

National Gambling Impact Study Commission-NGISC. Final Report. Washington D.C.: GPO, June 1999.

Nevada State Gaming Control Board. Nevada Gaming Abstract 2000. Carson City: Admin. NV GCB, December 2000.

---. Nevada Gaming Abstract 1999. Carson City: Admin. NV GCB, December 1999.

---. Nevada Gaming Abstract 1998. Carson City: Admin. NV GCB, December 1998.

---. Nevada Gaming Abstract 1997. Carson City: Admin. NV GCB, December 1997.

---. Nevada Gaming Abstract 1996. Carson City: Admin. NV GCB, December 1996.

Nevada State Gaming Control Board. Gaming Revenue Report 2000. Carson City: Admin. NV GCB, December 2000.

---. Gaming Revenue Report 1999. Carson City: Admin. NV GCB, December 1999.

---. Gaming Revenue Report 1998. Carson City: Admin. NV GCB, December 1998.

---. Gaming Revenue Report 1997. Carson City: Admin. NV GCB, December 1997.

---. Gaming Revenue Report 1996. Carson City: Admin. NV GCB, December 1996.

North, Douglass. Institutions, Institutional Change and Economic Performance. Cambridge: Cambridge University Press, 1990.

Pileggi, Nicholas. Casino. New York: Simon & Schuster, 1995.

Pine, Joseph and James Gilmore. The Experience Economy. Boston: Harvard Business School Press, 1999.

Pingle, Mark. U.S. Macroeconomic Statistics. New York: McGraw Hill, 2000.

Pommer, Matt. "Ho-Chuck Fear Impact of New Casino." Capital Times (Madison, Wisconsin), 23 November 2000.

Population of States on a Year-to-Year Basis. United States Census. 1 January 2002. http://eire.census.gov/popest/archives/state/st-99-3.txt

Reid, Ed, and Ovid Demaris. The Green Felt Jungle. Cutchogue: Buccaneer Books, 1963.

Rogin, Michael. Fathers and Children: Andrew Jackson and the Subjugation of the American Indian. New York: Knopf, 1975

Saum, Mary. "Native American Gaming: Will Organized Crime Organize on the Reservation?" Gaming Law Review 3-1 (1999): 49-59.

Sckolnick, Jerome. House of Cards. Boston: Little Brown and Company, 1978.

Seminole Tribe of Florida v. Butterworth 648 F.2d 310. 5th Cir Ct. 1981

Seminile Tribe of Florida v. Florida 517 U.S. 44, 116 Supreme Ct. 1114 1996.

Skibine, Alex. "Scope of Gaming, Good Faith Negotiations and the Secretary of Interior's Class III Gaming Procedures: Is IGRA Still a Workable Framework after Seminole?" Gambling Law Review 5-4 (2001): 401-413.

Spillman, Benjamin. "Prop1A Powers Casino Growth. Critics Decry Legal Oversight; Tribes favor Self-Regulation." Desert Sun [Palm Springs] 9 July 2000.

Stearns, John. "Tribal Casinos Gain Ground." Reno Gazette Journal 11 November 2001, E1.

Stein, Wayne. "Gambling: the Apex of a Long Struggle." Center for Native American Studies. Bozeman: Montana State University, February, 1997.

Structuring the Gaming Industry in the Public Interest. Cape Town: Corporate Image, 30 August 1996.

Taylor, Jonathan, Matthew Krepps and Patrick Wang. The National Evidence on the Socioeconomic Impacts of American Indian Gaming on Non Indian Communities-DRS001. Boston: Harvard University, Project on American Indian Economic Development, April 2000.

Thalheimer, Richard and Mukhtar Ali. "The Demand for Casino Wagering." University of Kentucky. Lexington: University of Kentucky, 30 May 2001.

Thompson, William. Legalized Gambling. 2nd Ed. Santa Barbara: A B C-CLIO, 1997.

Vervilos, Arkaterine. "Public Policy and the New Casino Gaming Markets." Thesis University of Nevada Reno, 1998.

Wait, Eugene. The Jackson Years. Huntington: Nova Science Publishers, 2000.

Wallace, Anthony. The Long, Bitter Trail: Andrew Jackson and the Indians. New York: Hill and Wang, 1993.

Willis, Lynda, comp. A profile of the Indian Gaming Industry-GAO-GGD 97-91. Washington DC: GAO, 5 May 1997.

Yamamura, Kevin "[California] State's Slot Machines are on the Rise" Bee Capital Bureau 27 December 2001.

Works Consulted: Law and Court Cases

Bryan v. Itasca County (426 U.S. S. Ct. 373, 392, 1976)

California Tribal State Gaming Compact

California v. *Cabazon* Band of Mission Indians (480 U.S. S. Ct. 202-1987)

Carroll v. State (361 FL S. Ct. So2d 144-1978)

Cherokee Nation v. Georgia (30 U.S. S. Ct. 1,5 Pet.1, 1831)

Cheyenne River Sioux Tribe v. South Dakota (93-1224, 8th Cir Ct. 93-1521-1993)

Citation Bingo LTD v. Otten (N.M. S. Ct. Lexis 426-1995)

Dellmuth v. Muth (491 U.S. 223, 227-28,105 L. Ed. 2d 181, 109 S. Ct. 2397-1989)

Florida Statute, Section 849.093

Hotel Employees & Restaurant Employees International Union v Gray Davis (21 Cal. S. Ct. 4th 585; 981 P.2d 990)

Indian Financing Act of 1974. 480 U.S. 202.218

Indian Gaming Regulatory Act of 1987-IGRA. Public Law 100-497. 17 October 1988

Iowa Mutual Insurance Company v. La Plante (107 S. Ct. 267; 93 L. Ed. 2d 244-1986)

Johnson v. M'Intosh (21 U.S. S. Ct. 543, 1823)

McClanahan v. Arizona State Tax Commission (411 U.S. S Ct. 164, 174-1973)

New Mexico v. Mescalero Apache Tribe (462 U.S. S. Ct. 324, 332-1983)

New Mexico ex. Rel Clark v. Johnson (N.M. S. Ct. Lexis; 904 p2d 11-1995)

Oregon Revised Statutes 167.117-20a

Oregon Revised Statutes 190.110-2

Organized Crime Control Act, 18 U.S.C. 1955

Ponca Tribe v. Oklahoma (37 F.3d 1422-1994)

Professional and Amateur Sports Protection Act-PAPSA (U.S.C. 3702-1994)

Public Law No. 83-280, 67 Stat. 588 (1953)

Rumsey Band of Wintun Indians v. Wilson (41 F.3d 431, 9th cir. 1994)

Seminole Tribe of Florida v. Butterworth (658 F. 2d 310 5th Cir. 1981)

Seminole Tribe of Florida v. Florida (517 U.S. 44, 116 S. Ct. 1114-1996)

Seminole Tribe v. Florida (91-6756, 1993 WL 475999-U.S. District Court, Southern District of Florida, 1993)

Spokane Tribe of Indians v. Washington (28 F.3d 991-1994)

State v. Appelbaum (366 FL S. Ct. So.2d 443-1979)

United States Constitution, U.S. House of Representatives. 1 September 2001 <HTTP://www.House.gov/Constitution/Constitution.html>

United States v. Mazurie (419 U.S. S. Ct. 544, 557-1975)

Washington v. Confederated Tribes of Colville Indian Reservation (447 U.S. 134, 154-1980)

White Mountain Apache Tribe v. Bracker, 448 U.S. S. Ct. 136, 143-1980

Williams v. Lee (358 U.S. S. Ct. 217 1959)

Worcester v. Georgia (31 U.S. S. Ct. 515, 6 Pet 350, 1832)

Made in the USA
Monee, IL
08 November 2026

67994722R00063